INTRODUCTION
TO DECORATING

Mary Gilliatt

INTRODUCTION TO DECORATING

Mary Gilliatt

Conran Octopus

First published in 1992 by Conran Octopus Limited
37 Shelton Street, London WC2H 9HN

Reprinted 1992

British Library Cataloguing in Publication Data
Gilliatt, Mary
    Introduction to Decorating
    I. Title
    643
    ISBN 1-85029-396-1

Project Editor Peggy Vance
Art Editor Ruth Prentice
Picture Researchers Abigail Ahern, Julia Pashley
Copy Editor Sarah Riddell
Proof Reader Andrew Steeds
Editorial Assistant Emma Wheeler
Production Serena Harrison, Alison McIver

DTP Ruth Prentice
Printed and bound in Singapore

CONTENTS

INTRODUCTION

*B*ecause I started my working life as a journalist and fell quite by accident into writing about design, then decorating and designing wallpapers and fabrics, I am inclined to think of myself as a design apologist – a sort of layman's interpreter of the intricacies of design and decoration. After all, I had to pick up my knowledge as I went along, just like any other person anxious to decorate their own home to the best of their ability. My confidence developed with practical experience and, through the study of books, magazines and other people's work, I learned to analyse why some rooms looked so much better than others.

Moreover, like a good many people who are interested *instinctively* in the process of creating comfortable, interesting and personal homes, I thoroughly dislike over-technical, over-complicated explanations and instructions clouding a subject which is inherently subjective.

All this has led me, still a reporter at heart, to write a number of books that explain all the various aspects of decorating in as clear a way as possible. In turn this occupation has afforded me particular advantages: the opportunity to see, at first hand, much of the best interior design around; to talk to all sorts of people of different ages, income groups and with varying tastes at design seminars and conferences around the world – to listen to their questions and hear their worries.

In this book it has been my aim to distil the wealth of information that I have been able to glean and present it in what I think is the most logical and helpful manner. I hope very much that it's useful to decorators at all levels.

WHAT IS *style?*

*B*efore you think about budgets, or colours, or almost anything else to do with decorating, you should really think about the question of style. For the style, or styles, you decide upon will dictate all your subsequent choices.

Unfortunately, the word 'style' resists easy definition, as does the word 'taste', with which it is often associated. When we describe someone as having 'style' or 'good taste' we are talking about a quality as difficult to define as perfect pitch. Whether it is in relation to clothes and accessories or furniture and possessions, it is a flair for putting things together in a way that is elegant, striking and individual.

The 'style' you choose for decorating and furnishing a particular room or a whole home, however, has a specific meaning. In this context, the term is used with reference to various broad categories to do with geographical location or architectural periods.

This chapter provides a definition of those categories of style which have, over the years, exerted the greatest influence on interior decoration.

LEFT: Formality and informality in an eclectic French room.
RIGHT: An exuberant mass of rich colour; comfortable clutter beneath a primitive frieze; utensils used as decoration.

First among these style categories are the 'national' styles: English, Italian, Japanese, Spanish, French, Scandinavian and the vaguer 'Oriental' styles. These divide into more specific styles like American Country, French Country, English Country or American South-West. There are also further terms, such as Urban, Beach House, Cabin or Ski Lodge, coined in response to the salient characteristics or ingredients that make them easy to recognize.

Some architectural and furnishing styles are directly associated with a particular age or epoch – Gothic; Renaissance; Commonwealth (British and American); Colonial Federal, and Greek Revival (American). Others are named after individual monarchs or regimes, for instance – Louis XIV, *Régence*, Louis XV, Louis XVI, Directoire and Empire in France; Tudor, Stuart, William and Mary, Queen Anne, early, mid and late Georgian,

TRADITIONAL: Old wooden doors, panelling, window embrasures and floorboards give a singularly mellow feel to this room. The effect is heightened by the worn steps leading up to a staircase door and the somewhat battered leather of the eighteenth-century chair with the same tortoiseshell tone as the pine.

Regency and Victorian in Britain and America; Gustavian in Sweden.

Several other style 'labels' also summon up distinct images of certain types of furniture and decoration. Seventeenth-century European Baroque, for example, was characterized by elaborate wood-carving and heavily ornamented furniture. Early eighteenth-century Rococo (which started in France) brought a taste for delicate mirrors and sconces, pastel colours, softly

romantic carvings and *boiserie* (carved panelling) with shells and foliage, cherubs and garlands. The eighteenth century in England is characterized by the great cabinet makers and designers – Chippendale, Sheraton, Hepplewhite and Adam – whose names are used to describe design styles that are as familiar in the United States as in Britain. The simple classical forms of the late eighteenth century echoed the architectural forms of ancient Greece and Rome, which continued to be a characteristic feature of Neoclassical style well into the early nineteenth century .

Biedermeier (named after the genial 'common man' of Austrian cartoons) was the term used for the ebony and honey-coloured, classically-inspired forms fashionable in Germany and Austria in the first half of the nineteenth century. Late nineteenth-century Art Nouveau, with its highly ornamental surfaces and its slight whiff of decadence, was followed in the 1920s and 1930s by Art Deco motifs, such as streamlined ladies, greyhounds and flowering columns. The stark modernity of the Bauhaus School was later to play a major part in the development of the modern International Style.

Well-known general terms – Traditional, Contemporary, Hi-Tech, Minimalist and Post-Modern – refer to various current styles of furnishing and decoration. Finally, there is Eclectic, a combination of any number of styles and periods, which is, for this reason, certainly the most popular, and generally the most interesting, of all styles.

MAKING CHOICES

Faced with such a bewildering array of possibilities, the question of which overall style to choose may at first seem daunting. In the end you

will have to decide what you are happiest with and what is most suitable for a particular house, apartment or lifestyle: it may even be a case of trying to identify some half-remembered mental picture of a room or rooms that you once liked. Design writers or designers often say, 'Just find the style that suits you best', but, without the chance to try out your ideas first, this is easier said than done. To try to shed at least some light on the subject, some brief descriptions follow of the more popular styles in current use.

TRADITIONAL

The term 'traditional' decorating conveys the *general* use of period designs (of whatever period) in furniture, fabrics, wallpapers, accessories and flooring, whether they are genuinely antique, inspired by antiques or careful replicas. Many people feel more secure gathering their ideas from the past, which has been tested, than experimenting with the products of the present. Traditional decorating should not, however, be simply an attempt to achieve more or less exact representations of a particular period: it is most successful when it combines the varied uses of traditional forms with the best contemporary materials and techniques.

TRADITIONAL COUNTRY

Over the last decade or so there has been a widespread fascination with the country furnishings of previous generations – particularly, but not exclusively, American, English, French and Scandinavian. The popularity of this type of decoration has been in part inspired by nostalgia for a romanticized rural past. Old country furniture and objects have been generally accessible and considerably cheaper than the more sophisticated furnishings of the same period, and their simplicity

11

and charm allows them to be mixed with modern furnishings to great effect. However, for those wanting to create rooms in a particular country style, a guide to the prominent characteristics of the most important of these follows.

AMERICAN COUNTRY has primitive furniture in sunwashed barn reds and dusty blues, or simple and spare Shaker furniture. Wide wooden floorboards are polished, painted, stencilled and often covered with rag rugs. There are old painted chests with folk-art motifs, quilts and four-poster beds (sometimes canopied), rocking chairs and kitchen chests or dressers. Checked cottons and small all-over motifs abound in fabrics. Stencilled motifs appear on floors, walls and furniture. There are also needlework samplers and turn-of-the-century Currier & Ives prints. Clapboard exteriors are as typical as slim vertical-boarded wainscoting within.

AMERICAN COUNTRY: Outdoor greens are gently repeated indoors in this charmingly airy bedroom. The green-painted bed between the windows (leading directly on to the porch) is complete with patchwork quilt and embroidered pillows. The miniature toy houses on the chest at the foot of the bed add a touch of whimsy.

AMERICAN SOUTH-WEST has Navajo Indian motifs on rugs, fabrics and wallpaper; they are also woven into Kelim-covered upholstery and cushions in colours based on the South-Western desert and mountain terrain – terracottas, sands and ochres, cerulean and washed-out blues, sage and pampas-grass greens, teals and firs. There are Indian artefacts, old Spanish silver and old blown green-tinged glass as well as rough-hewn furniture, leather-thonged chairs, terracotta tiles and conical chimneys in rough-cast plaster with rounded fireplaces and adobe-like structures.

ENGLISH COUNTRY is known for its understated elegance combined with, as the great English decorator John Fowler put it, a 'sense of shab'. Loose covers on upholstered pieces, mainly in chintz, have seen better days, as have the plaster walls and worn Oriental or needlework rugs on coconut, rush or sisal matting or on old wood or brick floors. The furniture is old pine, sometimes stripped or painted, and light mahogany; there are generous baskets of wood and antique paisley wool shawls casually thrown over gently threadbare sofas and chairs.

Grander English country houses have old Colefax & Fowler floral chintzes or faded linen prints; the window treatments are grander with swags and tails, and the polished mahogany or walnut furniture has become mellow with age. Walls are hung with sporting prints, political cartoons, a sprinkling of old family portraits and paintings of favourite horses and dogs; collections of family memorabilia are scattered everywhere. Dogs are stretched luxuriously in front of open log fires, blazing in defiance of the draughts and, at least in the rare hot days of summer, French windows are open, giving out upon lavender-fringed brick terraces.

Americans do not generally care for shabbiness, so their versions of English Country are invariably spankingly neat and fresh – and sometimes more comfortable, since Americans tend to be more concerned that their upholstered pieces are relaxing to sit or lounge on. Nevertheless, English upholstery is definitely becoming more comfortable and, besides, people may be wary about putting their feet up on obviously new or pristinely clean sofas and chairs. They need have no such scruples if the seating is somewhat battered and elderly.

FRENCH COUNTRY is a mixture of the provençale and the provincial. The hallmarks of the former are sharp small-scale cotton prints often bordered with brightly coloured or rich, dark backgrounds – intense yellow, bright green or cobalt blue, deep red and terracotta. Floors are laid with sun-baked terracotta tiles

VICTORIAN: Rich, dark green walls, comfortably upholstered tub chairs encircling a round gate-legged table, an old figured brass and fringed *gasolier* (a formerly gas-powered chandelier) and a tiled, Gothic design floor are all typical ingredients of the mid-Victorian era.

or flagged with stone, sometimes with straw or willow mats. Both French provincial and provençale furniture is simple, unsophisticated and somewhat primitive. Chairs typically have curved legs and cane seats with little tied-on seat cushions; tables, cupboards and dressers have serpentine-shaped tops and look somewhat rough-hewn. Provençale interiors give the impression of being sun-soaked throughout.

Other regions of the French countryside add different elements to the picture: small red and blue checks, bedrooms festooned with faded *toile de Jouy* cottons on the windows and beds, generous old elm or chestnut refectory tables, blue and white tiled kitchens, dark, low beamed ceilings and window-boxes full of brightly coloured geraniums and perlargoniums.

SCANDINAVIAN COUNTRY consists of sparse, uncluttered interiors. Wood is much in evidence, either unpainted, painted white (or another light colour), or in match-stick or tongue and groove boarding; beds are in alcoves, and there is stencilling on furniture, floors and walls. Colours are clear, bright and pastel; cottons are crisp and checked; lines are clean.

VICTORIAN

Queen Victoria's long reign (1837-1901) saw the emergence of a great diversity of styles, as extensive in the United States as in Britain. For in that vigorous, pulsating, industrial age were encompassed the revolution of steam and the inventions of sprung upholstery, proper plumbing, the motor car, the first electric light, as well as a vast new range of chemical dyes. This was a time when people wanted to advertise their new prosperity, believed in 'the more the better' and espoused

13

eclecticism. Styles ranged from the sturdy but elegant lines of the early Victorian interior, with its use of clear blues, light greens, lilacs and yellows, to the over-stuffed, richly coloured but dark rooms of the mid-Victorian period. Gothic, Rococo and Renaissance influences were followed by Scottish Baronial and Moorish tendencies, and the Arts and Crafts movement grew out of the impulse to harness the usefulness of mass-production to the forgotten skills of the craftsmen. In turn, these styles gave way to the Japanese-inspired Aesthetic movement, with its 'greenery-yallery' silks, peacock and sunflower motifs, whites and dove greys and collections of blue and white porcelain. Then came the 'sweetness and light' Queen Anne Revival, with its early eighteenth-century reproductions, gleaming silver and predilection for lace and atmosphere conducive to country-house parties. Finally, at the end of the Victorian period, there were the erotic and complicated vegetal convolutions of Art Nouveau Style.

And yet, despite this immense variety of styles, when we use the generic term 'Victorian style' – on both sides of the Atlantic, as well as in Australia and South Africa – what we generally think of is a mixture of all these characteristics. We imagine profusions of needlework rugs, sentimental prints and paintings, elaborate window treatments, occasional furniture, longcase (grandfather) clocks, big-game trophies, samplers, Moorish and Gothic motifs, bric-à-brac and the ubiquitous kerosene lamps.

Victorian furniture and objects, in all the different styles of the period, are still comparatively cheap. This to a large extent explains why Victorian style, in whatever manifestation, remains widely popular around the world.

LEFT: In this bathroom the absence of a lion's head spouting water, and the presence of the chrome towel rail and shaving mirror are the only faults in an otherwise perfect Neoclassical spoof.

CLASSICAL MOULDINGS (TOP TO BOTTOM): Cornice friezes displaying different ornamental motifs – festoons, dentil, greek key, egg and dart, acanthus – and, lastly, a winged sphinx.

NEOCLASSICAL

As with Victorian, what we call the Neoclassical embraces a variety of more specific styles, since different countries adapted it to suit their own tastes and requirements. Neoclassicism was the first real international style and was fully established in general design vocabulary by the end of the eighteenth century. It aimed to evoke the art and architecture of ancient Greece, Rome and, early in the nineteenth century, Egypt. Such aims had, of course, been expressed in Italy and other European countries since the Renaissance. Inigo Jones first introduced his style of Neoclassicism to England in the early seventeenth century; on his travels he had discovered Palladio's wonderful villas in the Italian Veneto as well as the great French Renaissance *châteaux* based on classical models. The styles became widely popular from the mid-eighteenth century, partly as a result of the archeological discoveries of Pompeii and Herculaneum as well as of various sites in Greece. These factors, together with the English aristocracy's habit of sending its scions on the Grand Tour of Europe, and, later, the deployment of large numbers of sailors and soldiers in the Napoleonic campaigns, spawned a variety of styles under the Neoclassical umbrella. They included Directoire and Empire in France, Regency in Britain, Federal, Greek Revival and, later, Empire in the United States, and Biedermeier in Germany, Austria and Scandinavia.

All these styles contribute to the general Neoclassical taste for stripes, tented ceilings, military symbols – crossed swords, spears, arrows and wreaths – shield-back chairs and military campaign furniture. Other features, taken directly from the ornamentation of classical architecture, include acanthus

16

leaves, Greek-key borders, the Greek honeysuckle 'anthemion', eagles, caryatids and lyre-backed chairs. Pilasters, pillars and columns, based on the classical orders, blend with Egyptian elements – languorous *chaises longues*, sphinxes, lions' paws, scrolled-back chairs and sofas – to create a composite of these classical ideas. These elements are complemented by muslin draperies, elaborate window treatments and fabric trims, marbles and *faux* marbles, and a lavish use of ebony, gilt, black and white.

COLONIAL

Although generally thought of as an American style, Colonial evokes the nineteenth-century European colonial experience too – stiflingly hot climates, verandas, mosquito-netted beds, slatted furniture, shutters, bare floorboards and light muslins.

American Colonial covers the period from the 1650s – when the early settlers, of necessity, had to make do with furnishings that were primitive, imported, or both – up to the late eighteenth century and Independence, when sophisticated and beautiful furniture and interiors were produced. Early regional variations in styles were a result of the settlers' different nationalities and of their former tastes and standards. The highly popular 'Colonial Revival' in the late nineteenth century has meant that many people today think of Colonial as a style which mixes American Country – with its painted wood panelling and stencilled folk art – with the fluted pilasters, Boston rocking chairs and Windsor chairs of early Federal.

CONTEMPORARY

Contemporary style means different things to different people. To some it means the Bauhaus-inspired International style of the late 1920s and early 1930s; to others, the brightly-coloured modern Italian furnishings of the Memphis school. To others it evokes the clean, unadorned lines and bare woods of the early Scandinavian style. In the strict sense of 'today's style', Contemporary style is perhaps best described as uncluttered Eclectic:

AMERICAN COLONIAL (LEFT): This room is a nice evocation of the American Colonial spirit. Its primitive paintings, dried flower garland, pine bench, longcase clock and drawn-thread linen tablecloth are the keynotes.

CONTEMPORARY (ABOVE): A comfortable mixture of furnishings in the kitchen-living room of a Long Island beach house, combining the vaguely old and the vaguely new with undoubted success. One could not help but feel relaxed and at home in such surroundings.

MODERN (RIGHT): The sitting room in designer Joseph's own home is elegantly spare, elegantly creamy and elegantly Art Deco.

LEFT: This bedroom experiments with different decorative ideas. It has an Empire feel, yet also incorporates elements of Edwardian Country.

each object or piece of furniture is given its own space; good modern upholstery is mixed with occasional antique pieces, used almost as sculpture, and stress is placed on objects being the best of their kind, or the best that can be afforded.

'SUITABILITY, SUITABILITY, SUITABILITY'

If a building is an excellent example of its period, or particularly well emulates the architecture of a specific era, you should remain sensitive to the general framework and proportions when furnishing and decorating. This does not mean that all the furnishings, colours, fabric and wallpaper designs (or reproductions) in an eighteenth-century house should be eighteenth century. People can become obsessed by the idea of achieving accurate period style; they forget that, if some of the comforts of the twentieth century had been available at the time, the people living then would have used them. After all, the furnishings of those times were determined by the uses to which rooms were then put.

Geographic location should play an equally large part in your choice of style. Houses in the sun need bright, cool colours and open and casual arrangements of furnishings and furniture. Rural houses and cottages usually dictate a more informal and unconventional approach than grander country houses, city apartments or town houses.

A SENSE OF STYLE

Some homeowners may have a particularly strong sense of what they want to achieve and a great deal of confidence in their own taste. They may aspire to create a rigorously modern effect in a seventeenth-century house, a Tudor scheme in a contemporary apartment building, or a nightclub venue in a country cottage. Nevertheless, the advice of Edith Wharton, the distinguished American author , is still valid: ' suitability, suitability, suitability'. This applies as much to the selection of an appropriate style as to the development of what is called an eye for detail.

Once you have gained some confidence about what is appropriate, you can then introduce the touches of originality that make a home quintessentially your own. The particular juxtaposition of colours and patterns, the lighting, the paintings and objects that you choose, the ways in which you arrange your possessions – all of these make for individual and memorable rooms. There is also felicitous serendipity, the sort of happy accident that suggests new colours, new ideas. A sweater left on a chair might introduce such a vibrant tone that you have to introduce something of that colour into the room – a pillow or a cushion, or perhaps a lamp; you might even make sure that you keep a bowl of flowers there. In much the same way as you occasionally see an article of clothing that you do not particularly need but that you know will make an uplifting difference to your wardrobe, so you might see a small piece of occasional furniture in a shop, an old shawl or throw, a print or painting, that you suddenly know will look just right. If you think of decorating like cooking a familiar dish to which you enjoy adding unexpected twists of flavours, you will very soon know instinctively what is best to do, and having done it, how to make it more distinctive. That is style, in every sense of the word.

The Personal Touch

✔ Unless you already prefer a certain style, how will you know which suits you best? Fortunately, there are certain criteria to follow. The first is to brush up your powers of observation. Really look at rooms that please you and try to analyse why they do. Is it the colours, the furniture, the arrangement, the fabric patterns or textures or the overall effect? Will the owners of these rooms be able to give any clue as to the style they adopted?

✔ Look through design books and magazines and make a note of further rooms you like. Tear pictures from magazines and file them. Study the captions to glean any crumbs of information. Look at room settings in stores, designer showcases and showhouses near you, as well as rooms set up in museums. Try to get hold of pictures of any rooms you particularly admire.

✔ Take notice of theatre, film and television sets and backgrounds. Which architectural styles and which types of buildings give you most pleasure? Do you prefer old houses or new ones with clean, modern lines, memorable designs, or plain comfortably anonymous objects?

✔ Decide if you are happier with formal or informal styles. Will the style you choose depend on the room to be decorated? This will affect your choice of furnishings. Some styles are casual and informal, whereas period styles and most traditional furnishings (except upholstery) are rather more formal.

IN THE
beginning

*O*nce you have decided on the most appropriate style for your home, or room, the next step is to create the basic framework on which the whole design must hang. For whatever mood or detailing you have chosen will only function to its best advantage provided you have come to terms with the space in hand. You therefore have to think about what you have available, how you can improve it, how best you can apportion it, and what you should do about lighting, ceilings, walls, floors, woodwork and windows. Only then can you think about furnishings and the final arrangements.

It is, of course, important to bear in mind that successful interior design is as much about practicality and comfort as it is about mood and style – although you should certainly not lose sight of the direction in which you want to go. Nevertheless, however beautiful the window treatments, however original the colour schemes and splendid the furnishings, none of it will matter if the overall room is not comfortable to live in and if, at the bottom line, the space does not really work.

LEFT: The cut-out circles of the door are satisfyingly echoed in the rounded foreground shapes.
RIGHT: Strong lines of fireplace and beams are emphasized by a two-tone colour scheme; bookshelves and glass table 'float' over the floor; deep shelves surrounding the door heighten perspective.

Clearly, whatever the scale of the undertaking, it is wise to draw up a plan of action rather than to attack the project in a piecemeal way. To do this, you will first have to have a good idea of how you would most like to live in the space and what you would be comfortable spending to arrive at that optimum state. Since your budget, the time you have at your disposal and the way you would most like to live very seldom coincide, it is sensible to outline the eventual goals and to work backwards from there. This is as good a way as any of getting priorities right from the start. And it helps to formulate sensible, staged plans so that you can decide what you *have* to spend money on and where you can make compromises for the time being.

To get your priorities in order, start by asking yourself the following set of questions:

• What is the state of walls, woodwork, ceilings and windows in the room or rooms you are intending to decorate, or redecorate? If there are damp stains, cracks on walls and ceilings, or ill-fitting windows, they absolutely must be seen to.

•How new is the wiring in the house or apartment? If you add any new outlets or points, will they overload the system or will they be difficult to install? Is the wiring up to code requirements and adequate for your present needs? Do you have enough outlets or points in the right places for maximum flexibility (in corners, behind beds, within easy reach of seating – so that you do not get a trail of wires across the floor – or above the working surfaces in a kitchen)?

•Would it be an immense improvement to install better doors or longer or more graceful French windows anywhere (provided they do not look odd from the outside)?

•Do you think you need to add any

LEFT: In this airy country room, simple forms, organic hues and textures do not distract the eye from the strong structural rhythm of the ceiling beams.

BELOW LEFT: The spaciousness of the garden extends into the house through the use of vibrant colours and floral prints.

BELOW: The warm, plain tones of this cottage interior emphasize the earthy texture of the wall.

architectural details to a room or rooms? Sometimes a handsome cornice, a dado, a pediment over a door or another fireplace will make an enormous difference, often out of all proportion to the expense. Even if you cannot afford plaster, or the cheaper and lighter polystyrene or fibreglass mouldings, you can still achieve a much more distinguished look with paper borders.

• Are radiators or air conditioning units unsightly? If so, can they be resited, improved or disguised? What is the existing hardware like, door handles, light switches, dimmer switches, finger plates, taps and so on? Could they do with replacing, rebrassing or just cleaning and polishing? This might sound pernickety in the grand scheme of things, but it is these minor details

that can spoil new decorative schemes and wreck budgets if there need to be changes later.

• What is the kitchen like? Are appliances in good working order and likely to last several years before they will need to be replaced? What are the units like? Ugly units might look much better with new hardware and a coat of paint. Working, but unattractive appliances can also be re-enamelled.

• What about the plumbing? Could you fit in another bathroom, shower room or powder room? If so, how much will it cost? (Putting in another bathroom at the outset will add to the general comfort and should also make your home a more attractive proposition when it comes to reselling – again, out of all proportion to the initial cost.) Do shabby existing features really need to be replaced or can they be resurfaced?

• Do you need to put in burglar, fire and smoke alarms? (This is often a condition of insurance coverage; if so, they will definitely have to be installed right away.)

• What about the flooring? Floorboards under the existing carpet or vinyl covering can be scraped, sanded, stained, painted or polished. What would a different kind of floor (ceramic, quarry tiles, marble, sisal, new vinyl or carpet) do to your budget?

• What about storage? Is it adequate or will you need to fit in more, if not right now, later? And is there room?

If any of these questions reveal the need for structural work – rewiring, replumbing, reflooring, repairing damaged walls, ceilings or floorboards, replacing or putting in new windows, replacing or resurfacing bathroom or kitchen fixtures – this must be done before any decoration is started. Equally, it must be included in the overall budget, just as you must allow for any extra storage and carpentry or joinery.

23

SOUND BUDGETING

To form a realistic budget with which you feel comfortable, you should ask yourself these questions:

• What do you feel is the most you can spend right now on the project, bearing in mind that you should always keep a contingency sum in reserve for emergencies? Can you spend more money at a later period? If so, when? (This should help you to formulate a staged plan.)

• Is your budget figure realistically based on current prices? Have you researched current prices for merchandise and services, or is it just guesswork? It is essential that you look into the cost of everything you need and would like to do. If you have no real idea of present-day prices your budget might be seriously misleading.

• If you do not really need to have any *structural* work done, and are not sure what your *decorating* priorities should be, it might help to work out a list of the ten luxuries or improvements that you think would make your home look and work better. For example, if you work all day but like to cook, would a particularly efficient refrigerator/ freezer, oven/hob or microwave be priorities for your kitchen? Do you think a Jacuzzi in your bathroom would help you unwind? Would you like to make your home look more distinctive by adding architectural details, a better fireplace or some period mouldings?.

Having gone through these two groups of questions you will be thinking realistically about your home. The questions might sound elementary, but in the enthusiasm, nervousness or confusion of the moment it is all too easy to forget the most basic elements. Moreover, unless you answer these questions, and cost the answers, you cannot possibly form a proper budget.

HOW TO DRAW UP A FLOOR PLAN

Accurate floor plans, quite apart from their usefulness for working out any changes, will be invaluable for deciding on furniture arrangements later (see also practical tips on pp. 130–3).

The best way to start is by making a large sketch of one of your rooms – say the living room. For this operation, and the subsequent floor plan proper, you will need the following:

✔ Some sheets of graph paper (paper divided into small squares)
✔ Some sheets of blank white paper (in case you make a mistake)
✔ Two well-sharpened pencils (3H and H)
✔ An eraser, a set square, and a ruler
✔ A good-size retractable tape-measure

Think first about your room. Is it rectangular? Square? Irregular? Draw its shape out as generously as you can on one of the sheets of paper. After you have made this preliminary sketch of your room, and you are satisfied that it accurately reflects its shape, take the tape-measure and measure the following: the length of the walls; the width of the doors and any openings; the width of windows and any fixtures such as radiators, built-in closets, bookcases and so on; the thickness of any partitions; the distance of fittings from one another; the positions of electrical outlets, telephone and TV sockets, radiators, grilles, other permanent heating appliances and any air conditioning units. Mark all these clearly on the *sketch* of your room, using the symbols (shown on pp. 132–3) for all these services and architectural elements. This will serve as your source of reference for your completed floor plan.

To draw up the plan proper, you must first decide on the scale and then duplicate the room's exact proportions on your plan. For example, if you have a rectangular room, and the long walls happen to be twice the length of the short walls, then the long lines on your sketch plan representing the long walls should be twice the length of the lines representing the short walls.

Most designers work on a scale of 2 cm to 1 m (about ¼ in to 1 ft) so that if a wall is 3.5 m (approximately 12 ft) long, you should draw a line 7 cm long. If you always use graph paper on the appropriate scale, it will be very easy to draw up the scale plan of any room. But if, for any reason, you do not have any graph paper at hand at the time you need it, you can still draw a room to scale by drawing in a basic grid. If you are drawing up a room where literally every centimetre counts (for example, a kitchen, laundry room or bathroom), it is often preferable to use a larger scale .

MAKING AN ACCURATE ROOM PLAN

Now take your sharp pencils, eraser and ruler (unless you have the type of graph paper with invisible perforations that allows you to draw impressively straight lines without a guide) and draw the perimeter of your room to the chosen scale. It is important to do this absolutely accurately, so work on a smooth, flat surface, preferably a drafting board, securing your graph paper to the board with drafting tape (which is better than masking tape because you can pull it off the paper after use without fear of leaving a mark).

Gently erase any door openings, marking their clearance, or swing, when opened, with an arc.

DRAWING A FLOOR PLAN

Before you attempt to draw an accurate floor plan, you should first make a rough sketch plan of your room, or rooms, marking in any windows, doors, radiators, excrescences, electrical outlets, and TV points.

Measuring for Moving

It is important to take measurements of front doors, windows and staircases (especially the width, height and depth of any turns in the stairwell, or of any lift in an apartment building) to make sure there is room for large pieces of furniture – sofas, pianos, oversize armchairs, desks, bookcases, dressers, and so on – to be moved successfully into a new home.

Checklist

✔ What are the essential things to be done to make your home work and look better?

✔ What is the minimum that needs to be spent?

✔ Where can you make savings?

✔ Can you form a reasonably long-term plan so that urgent things can be implemented now, others later?

✔ Can you make sensible compromises? For instance, once you are in a position to buy better things, can you 'recycle' some of your older possessions to other rooms, say, a porch or hall?

Designers and architects usually mark doors like this. Then mark in windows, radiators, electrical outlets, TV points, sockets and so on (using the symbols shown on pp. 130–1 as a guide), just as you did with your sketch plan. (The 3H pencil is useful for this, since it can be sharpened to a very precise point. But remember to draw lightly, because its hardness makes it difficult to erase.) The sample grid illustrated on pp. 132–3 will give you an idea of how you should proceed.

Add in any other fixtures or odd corners, breaks or excrescences, again making sure that everything is strictly accurate. This constant stressing of accuracy may be tiresome, but the slightest deviation could have disastrous consequences when it comes to adding furniture or fitted furniture.

EMPLOYING HELP

If your rooms require major work which you feel unable to tackle yourself, you will need the help of a contractor, probably followed by a curtain maker and an upholsterer, in addition, possibly, to an architect or interior designer or both..

Of course, if you hire architects and/or interior designers, they will almost certainly recommend contractors and tradespeople they are generally used to working with and can presumably trust. With any kind of big contracting job they will draw up specifications for all the work needed and put the job out to tender, complete with marked-up plans. They will then choose what they consider to be the best bid, which will not necessarily be the cheapest but will, with any luck, be the fairest.

If the professionals you hire have to work far from their usual locality, they will probably have to make enquiries about contractors and other specialists in the area. It will be their responsibility to find suitable people, unless you are in a position to suggest names you have heard to be good and reliable. Your responsibility is to find the right architect or designer in the first place.

FINDING AND WORKING WITH AN ARCHITECT

Probably the best way to find an architect is through personal recommendation so that you can see his or her work for yourself. If you know no one who has recently had a home successfully built, renovated or extended, find out the names of architects whose work you have liked from magazines, newspapers or books. Your local university or college department of architecture may be a good source for referrals, or you could ask the advice of an architectural acquaintance (on the

whole it is best not to commission a friend). The main professional architectural association in the country (for example, the RIBA in Britain and the AIA in the United States) may be able to suggest some names in your area whose work you can then arrange to see. Satisfied clients are usually willing to show off their houses, and the architects will always be happy to supply photographs and arrange appointments. There is nothing to stop you employing an architect from the

area of your choice, but remember the advantages of a local architect: familiarity with local contractors and the foibles of local inspectors, more regular supervision of the work in progress and, not least, expenses which will do much less damage to your bank account.

Many would argue that it is quite difficult to persuade an architect to take on renovation work if nothing additional is required, since most members of the profession, unless they are desperate for commissions,

26

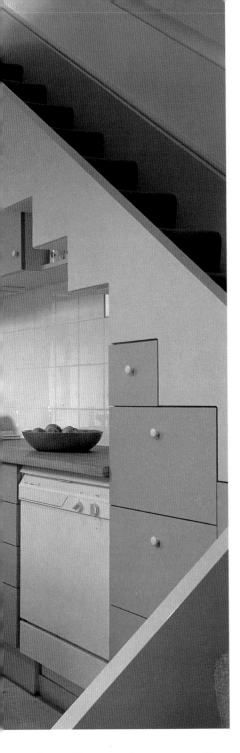

KEYING DESIGN TO ARCHITECTURE: The spatial planes provided by the strong angles and zigzags of the staircase, the deep window embrasures, the ceiling beam and island unit inspire much of the decoration in this galley-kitchen neatly tucked into a hall-stairway area. Aquamarine-painted cupboards and drawers neatly alternate with white tiles and appliances, while butcher-block counter tops offer a tonal counterpoint.

would rather concentrate on more ambitious projects. On the other hand, many young architects are often only too glad to take on small jobs and prove their mettle. Also, larger firms often make a practice of taking on a certain number of renovations a year. Equally, of course, if the work is not very major, you might well persuade an architect to provide a partial service which will consist of providing sketch plans and ideas, but not necessarily any supervision or more detailed work.

In any event, whoever you choose will certainly discuss his or her method of charging at your first meeting. If not, you should bring it up so that both sides can be quite clear about what is expected. Normally, architects will charge a percentage on the cost of larger jobs, an hourly fee on smaller renovations and an agreed fee for drawings and plans. Do not be surprised if you are charged more when you change your mind about ideas and projects. But, equally, do not allow yourself to be bullied. It is your home, you are going to live in it, and there are very few people who know precisely what they want right from the beginning.

FINDING AND WORKING WITH AN INTERIOR DESIGNER

Pretty much the same advice and strictures apply to the hiring of an interior designer. Many people feel that employing a designer is an expensive luxury, and certainly I spend much of my life writing books and trying to demonstrate that it is perfectly possible, given the inclination, to go it on your own. In many cases, however, especially where a straightforward renovation or spatial alteration project is concerned, a designer will be able to save you the services of an architect as well as helping you with interior design ideas and schemes.

The Case for Employing a Designer

✔ A good designer should be able to save you money in the long term by preventing expensive mistakes as well as reducing the confusion and stress involved in the project.

✔ A sympathetic and informed outsider will bring fresh insights into the design of your home and will suggest ways to make your rooms function efficiently and look their best.

✔ He or she will: use fabrics, papers and floor coverings that you will rarely find in a retail stores; design things specially for you; supervise contractors, curtain-makers, carpenters, floor layers; help find furniture and accessories, and generally relieve you of the tedious and nerve-wracking chores.

✔ A professional designer will recognize that it is your home, your money, and that many clients have excellent ideas of their own but simply lack the time, inclination or contacts to carry them out.

✔ Most important of all, a good designer should be prepared to work within your budget, and, if you are not sure about the money that is required, will help you honestly to price your requirements.

27

Designers' fees vary considerably, as do their methods of charging – depending upon the scope of the work and its location. Some designers charge a percentage of the whole job. A designer might say, 'My terms are 10% handling charge added to everything, whether in the form of services (like contractors' charges), goods (furnishings, art, accessories) or expenses.' If this is so, you should ascertain whether they are putting the 10% on to trade or to retail prices which will clearly make a difference.

Another method is to charge a retainer or design fee and to split trade discounts with the customer or client. In this event, a designer may say: 'My minimum or standard retainer or design fee is such and such, but I am willing to split my trade discount with you and charge you 20% on trade prices.' Since trade prices are anything from one third to 40% off retail, this means you will be paying a design fee for the designer's services, but getting some 15 to 20% off retail prices. Interestingly, customers are often better off with this method than they are taking the full retail route whereby the designer charges no fee and simply takes the difference between trade and retail.

Yet another method – which I happen to like because both parties then know exactly where they are – is to charge an agreed design fee or retainer and hand over all the designer discounts to the customer with a small handling charge on top. This way the customer can see how much he or she has been saved, which is often considerably more than the design fee. Some designers charge an initial consultancy fee for advice and ideas, and then, once they have a contract, remove the consultancy fee from the overall price. This is a good way of getting over the unfair practice (in which,

alas, all too many clients indulge) of making a designer go to endless lengths to produce schemes and then taking the schemes to some younger, more inexperienced and cheaper designer to carry out – or just using the unfairly extracted schemes themselves. Other designers charge so much a room or so much an hour plus, of course, materials and labour. It's a field that is full of variables, so do find out charges and methods of working right from the beginning.

FINDING AND WORKING WITH A CONTRACTOR

If you decide that you do not need the services of an architect or designer, but definitely need a contractor, you may approach the whole task of finding one with some trepidation. Bitter tales about frightening incompetence, bad workmanship, hopeless timekeeping and gross overcharging are so rife that it is worth stating that good, careful, conscientious and reasonable contractors do in fact exist – especially in small family firms where members of a family enjoy working together, are often very versatile in their skills, can be elastic about hours and take pride in maintaining their reputation.

As always, personal recommendation is one of the best ways, especially if other people's experiences have been fairly untraumatic. Local builders' merchants and good hardware or paint stores, who after all supply a great many contractors, are usually willing to make suggestions, as are local architects, structural engineers and surveyors of friendly disposition. Once again, it is a good idea to check with the relevant trade association or federation, as many of these bodies keep a directory of accredited names.

When you have assembled a list of possibles, ask three contractors at

RIGHT: The blue pole-beams in this utility room are practical and decorative. They provide drying space for clothes and linens, but also serve as a distinctive design feature in their own right. The effect is similar to that of a boat-house with oars on racks. The table lends continuity to this simple room.

least to come and inspect the house or apartment and give each one a copy of your specific requirements, along with the plans (drawn up as suggested on pp. 24–5). On receiving their bids or estimates, fend off the natural inclination to accept the cheapest (unless all are very close in price, or you have heard particularly good things about one of them). A low sum might betray a builder more concerned to land the contract than to follow up with a job well done, quite apart from the fact that work done on the cheap almost always has to be done again within a short time and so will turn out to cost you more in the long run.

Examine the different bids closely. For example, do they all specify the same number of paint coats (if you failed to give a number in your specification)? Are you sure that they have all estimated for precisely the same amount of work and materials? Have any of them made suggestions for an improvement over and above the specification? If so, have they given reasons for its inclusion? Compare all the different provisional costs for intangibles

OPEN-PLAN LIVING: In this all-in-one eclectically furnished living area different 'rooms' are visually defined and separated. Marginally different levels, columns and over-sized pots of plants all substitute very well for more conventional walls. This method preserves the lightness, airiness and unity of the space without in any way confusing its various functions.

(like finding and curing the cause of damp patches). Any conditions in small print on the back of the bids should be thoroughly read and understood. For example, there might be denials of obligation if workmen break something or cause damage to your property.

If the final sums quoted are all much of a muchness, be guided by factors such as: which firm gives the earliest and most realistic date for completion; which firm will subcontract less work out; which personalities seem the most conscientious and considerate.

One further point: if you have an old house, do make sure that you are employing people who have proven experience with old structures and are sensitive to their quirks and failings. A builder who has only dealt with new, or newish, buildings will rarely be as ingenious as someone steeped in preserving and adapting the old.

Remember to visualize every room in its entirety, from base or skirting boards to mouldings and hardware. State where cracks have to be filled, old flaky paint and paper removed and how many coats of paint you want, giving the type of paint (matt, semi-gloss, eggshell, gloss – whether oil- or water-based – and, if you know them at this stage, the colours and numbers). If you want walls papered, decide whether you also want them lined first and note where you want borders applied as well. State which pipes you want concealed or boxed-in, which partition walls you want removed, and the measurements of any appliances or fixtures you want installed. Say exactly where you want cupboards, bookshelves and shelves built; give precise dimensions, marking positions of new carpentry work on the plans. (You should already have discussed all these matters *in situ* with the various contenders.) Also show on the plans exactly where all light fixtures and outlets should go, where light switches should be placed and which lights they control. (A frequent mistake is for people to specify that they want only table lamps and uplights and to forget completely that they would like to be able to switch some of them on from the wall.)

Even if the list seems enormous and takes a great deal of time, the amount of money and frustration it will save in the long run will be well worth it. It is so easy for the amateur to forget really quite obvious and necessary items, the cost of which can mount up over and above the original estimates to create nasty financial shocks for which there is no redress at all.

You should provide contractors with separate decoration schedules too, giving ceiling, wall, moulding, floor and woodwork treatments for each room under separate headings. Without knowing your preferences, contractors are inclined to give provisional figures for the kind of decoration they think you will like. If the builder makes a mistake, all you have to do is show him a copy of your original specification and he will have to make good his error. Make sure you have plenty of copies: one each for you and the contractor, one to pin up in each room, and one for the master file.

KEEPING A CHECK

However diligently you have prepared your specifications and decorating schedules, you may well find that extras still pop up. You will suddenly think of a different solution to a problem; some new material or pattern will catch your eye; a window will have to be replaced, or some other feature altered. Hence you must try to keep a contingency sum in reserve for changes of mind as well as for emergencies. In an old house, for example, disturbance by work in progress might well reveal all sorts of hitherto unsuspected faults which, even if you had an engineer's report, might not have been discovered.

If the job is sizeable, try to have a meeting with the contractor at least once a week, to go over every room. Take down in writing any new decisions and any criticisms made, date and initial your notes and send a copy of them to the contractor as well as filing a copy yourself. Even when you think you completely trust your contractor, it is still wise to keep a check on things. When it comes to the crunch, you are the only person entirely dedicated to your interests.

Usually contractors ask for a third or even half the estimated sum for the work before they start, and the rest in staged payments. Make sure you resist any pressure to settle your final account until you are sure that every detail is completed *to your satisfaction*. It will not endear you to the contractor, but it is your only safeguard.

31

Preparing a Specification

✔ A clearly presented specification is the key to any successful job. It should be concise, decisive and detailed so that contractors have no need to ask for explanations, take decisions on their own or have any leeway whatsoever for misunderstandings.

✔ To help you in the preparation of an accurate document you should write down: any work a structural engineer or surveyor has told you should be done; any work that your mortgage company or bank insists should be done; any work you must carry out to qualify for a grant (in the case of an old building); all the improvements you want to make yourself.

✔ When you are satisfied that you have written down absolutely everything that you want and have to have done, it is advisable to divide up the work into what needs to be done on the exterior, and what should be done on the interior, room by room and floor by floor. Put the plumbing, electrical and masonry work under separate headings, since these are different trades and might be subcontracted. You could do the same for all the carpentry and tiling, as much to keep tabs for yourself on all the jobs as to help the contractor.

THE DESIGN
ingredients

*O*nce you feel that you have organized the basics – that is, you know what you are going to do in outline, who is going to do it, and more or less exactly how much it is going to cost – you can start to finesse those somewhat intangible, but extremely important elements of a room's design that give it its initial character. These are the design 'ingredients', to use a cooking metaphor, of colour, light, pattern and texture which must all be blended subtly together so that each will enhance the others to create a harmonious whole.

This might sound abstract; it *is* rather abstract when you write or say it. But when you start to think how much difference light (whether natural or artificial) makes to colour, how completely colour can alter the look of a pattern, how much texture alters the look of a colour, indeed, how much light can alter texture, and how much texture too can change a pattern, you will begin to see how inextricably they are all combined. Imagine then the infinite number of changes you can make to a colour scheme simply by altering the various combinations.

LEFT: Brilliant colours bring old panelled rooms into the late twentieth century with the speed of light.
RIGHT: The interplay of colour, light, pattern and texture focuses the eye and produces these unusual but harmonious effects in a hallway, bedroom and sitting room.

SIMPLE DEMONSTRATIONS

As an experiment, take a piece of fabric, of any colour, and hold it up to a window in daylight. Then, with the curtains or blinds drawn, shine a light on the same piece of fabric and see the difference in the tones. Again look at a fabric or wallpaper pattern in one colourway, say, blue, and then look at the same pattern in another, say, rose. Notice how different they look. Put the blue colourway against a blue background, then against a rose background both by day and by night, and again compare the difference.

Now take a piece of, say, cream velvet; then put it beside cream linen, cream muslin, cheesecloth, a bit of cream Berber carpet, creamy sisal matting or a cream china cup. See how very different the same colour looks in varying textures. Finally, shine a light from a torch straight on to a piece of carpet or tweed; then angle the torch so that the light hits the texture from the side. Even if you were not consciously aware of the effects before, you will certainly see now how all these elements interact with each other and how the *way* they are put together uniquely changes a room.

UNDERSTANDING COLOUR

Colour is to rooms what light is to daytime. It is also the quickest, easiest and cheapest way to give character to a space – or to change its existing character. The trouble is that, although colour sounds an undemanding, even frivolous, subject, it is in fact hugely complex, with not only a great many complicated psychological and emotive overtones, but its own vocabulary of well-defined terms. It is worth studying the vocabulary and colour wheel (see opposite). They might seem dull, but, once learned, they

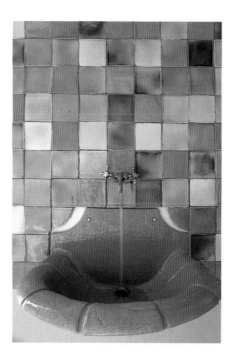

A patchwork of tiles forms a bright background for the mango-coloured washbasin with handsome old brass taps.

will not only make you look at colours differently, but will stand you in good stead when you try to devise interesting colour schemes for your rooms.

FINDING INSPIRATION

One of the most enduring and enlightening books on the subject (*On the Law of Simultaneous Contrast of Colours and Matching of Coloured Objects*) was written in the nineteenth century by the Frenchman, M.E. Chevreul. Having worked in the great Gobelins tapestry factory in France, he made the discovery that colours interact in unexpected ways. He noticed that red threads next to blue or green looked quite different from red threads next to yellow or white; and that white or black, set beside primary colours such as red and yellow, made them look correspondingly lighter and brighter, or darker and richer. His theories had a particular application to art and had a great influence on many painters, most notably the

Impressionists. Chevreul observed that once painters had patiently absorbed his various colour rulings and had learned to break down everything they saw into tones and half tones, light and shade, they invariably painted to far greater effect. The same is true in decoration. Once you have learnt closely to observe the varying colours in anything that pleases you, especially in nature, you can manipulate colours for rooms in a more confident way.

Picture the countryside in the early summer, next a rain-starved desert terrain, and then a sky- or seascape. Most rural landscapes contain a patchwork of greens set against blue, with accent colours provided by flowers and blossoms, bark and bare earth. The desert, in contrast, has tones of soft ochre and browny terracotta, grey greens (of cacti) and the sun-filled cerulean of sky. Similarly, in sky- or seascapes, depending upon the time of day, there is an extraordinary range of blues, blue greens, aquamarines and whites, with accent notes from rocks, beach, boats and birds. At sunset, on a clear, warm night, there will be the deep navy of the ocean, and the great splashy sky full of violet, apricot, rose, orange and yellow.

EMOTIVE RESPONSES

Once you have learnt to break colours down, the extraordinarily violent responses that some people have to a given colour seem all the more illogical. 'I cannot *stand* blue,' someone will say. But if you think of blue in all its manifestations, you might visualize forget-me-nots and periwinkles, the fresh violet blue of hyacinths and bluebells, the intense cerulean blue of delphiniums and Morning Glory and the gentle faded quality of hydrangeas and lavender, wistaria and lupins. Then there are

THE COLOUR WHEEL

Colour Inspirations

✔ Whatever colour you choose to think about will inevitably give rise to a host of evocative associations.

✔ The pinks, crimsons, lacquer-reds and scarlets of wild poppies and mallows; the clear and dark reds of tulips, scarlet lobelias and dahlias, pinky-red bergamots and fuchsias, rose and scarlet geraniums and pelargoniums; the purpled reds of peonies; the whole gamut of reds and pinks of roses from velvety hybrids to the delicate shell-pink of hedge varieties; raspberries, strawberries, mulberries and loganberries, hips and haws, cherries and rosy apples; red peppers and cayenne, paprika and the warm yellowy-rose of papayas. The reds of Oriental rugs and Chinese lacquer, rubies and garnets; terracottas and bricks and the rose-reds and blood-reds of sunsets.

✔ The fresh, zinging yellows of daffodils and jonquils, tulips and polyanthus, crocuses and buttercups, dandelions and chrysanthemums; the intense centres of daisies and wild irises; the paler yellows of primroses and freesias, honeysuckle and yellow shrub roses; the yellows of lemons and ripe pears, peppers and corn on the cob; the rosy yellow of apricots and the greeny-yellow of olive oil; ripe corn fields and corn stubble; hay and blonde hair; butter and Devonshire farm cream; sand and clay; ochre and burnt sienna; amber and cornelian; butterflies and the stripes of bees and wasps; canary feathers and parrots; marmalade and ginger cats; and ginger and saffron, curry and saffron robes.

It is easier to understand colour and harmony, if you think in terms of the colour wheel which, in its most basic form, consists of the three primary colours: yellow, red, and blue. A mixture of any two primaries produces a secondary colour: orange (red + yellow), green (yellow + blue) or purple (blue + red). All colours are formed by mixing varying quantities of the three primaries, to which may be added the non-colours: black and white. 'Tints' are lighter versions of colours produced by mixing them with white and 'shade' are darker versions produced by mixing them with black.

Quite apart from these colours and their tints and shades there are 'neutral' colours which, taken literally, mean tones of grey formed either by mixing varying quantities of black and white or equal quantities of the primaries: yellow, red and blue. In terms of interior design, however, neutrals also include browns, beiges, creams, and off-whites.

Pattern is piled on pattern, texture on texture, overlaid with different colours so that you hardly know where one object begins and another ends in this French living room.

all the blues of the sky: the pale, blue-grey dawn, the azure of a hot summer's day, the grapey blue of impending storms, the deep, velvet damson-blue of a sultry night. Conjure up too the blues of sun-dazzled water and the various precious and semi-precious stones: limpid, translucent aquamarines; deep, dark sapphires; the gaiety of turquoise, and the intensity of lapis lazuli and bluejohn. How can any-body, given this extraordinary variety, still make such sweepingly negative statements? Of course, when you *do* think of colours as they are revealed in all their natural hues and tones, it becomes easy to translate them into interesting monochrome schemes, applying dif-ferent shades to the various furnish-ings that go to make up a room – curtains, carpets, chairs, pillows, sofas, wallpapers and accessories.

COLOURS AND STYLE

There are, of course, a number of colours which have particular asso-ciations with certain periods, styles and even designers. For instance, one immediately connects pale rose, off-whites, blues and greens with Rococo and the eighteenth century; rich red stripes and yellow and blue brocades and damasks with French *Empire* and Regency; dusty and intense Williamsburg blues, varia-tions of barn red, and a sage Adam green with Colonial and Federal; deep, dark reds and greens, blues and a good deal of chocolate brown with the mid and late Victorian periods; greens and yellows with the Aesthetic movement; white, white and white again with the Modern movement.

TOP RIGHT: The cool white of the overmantle and dado and the marble of the mantle-piece itself form a counterpoint to the deep crimson of the walls.
CENTRE RIGHT: Yellow-painted panelling and wide pine floorboards complement the Chippendale-style chairs in this handsome American room.
BOTTOM RIGHT: Only the green plants provide contrast in this monochrome scheme.

Other colours have different historical links. Chinese red and Ming blue are the distinctive colours of Chinese lacquer and ceramics exported to the West in the late seventeenth and early eighteenth century; Etruscan and Pompeiian colours include a special terracotta red; and imperial purple and royal blue were given regal praenomens because they were as rare as gold in classical times (the one derived from millions of molluscs, the other from lapis lazuli).

Nevertheless, one should not feel too strictly tied to authenticity when trying to use colours to recreate a particular style of period. I mentioned earlier that a number of twentieth-century features and refinements would doubtless have been incorporated into earlier styles had they then existed; in the same way, it must be remembered that there was a very limited choice of colour available to people until the invention of chemical and aniline dyes in the mid-nineteenth century.

Fabrics from English companies such as Bennison and Hodsoll McKenzie, printed in faded colours on beigy linen and cotton, are made to *look* charmingly old, but, of course, nothing ever started off looking comfortably mellow and faded. All old fabrics were originally bright and clear, so these new 'old-looking' fabrics are really a short cut to the fashionable look of 'benign neglect' or 'shabby chic' for furnishings that appear to have been around in the family for a good long time. Still on the subject of old fabrics, or at least old designs, companies such as Liberty, Sanderson, Colefax & Fowler, Scalamandré, Coutan & Tout, Brunschwig & Fils, Clarence House, Fortuny and the Victorian specialists Watts & Co. all produce and/or sell deliciously coloured modern variations of old textile

documents. It is an interesting fact that people rarely, however, demand the original colouring. In short, as always, choose colours you feel most comfortable with and which seem most appropriate to the atmosphere and situation of your home.

BALANCING AND MANIPULATING COLOURS

If you have not really thought much about colour before, how will you be able to recognize the colours with which you will feel most comfortable? This sounds rather like asking somebody how they know what they like (which, as with all instinctive responses, many people find extremely hard to answer).

There is no doubt that being able to balance colours one against another in a subtle way, like the ability to balance tastes and proportions, is a useful skill. Fortunately, it is a skill that is not too difficult to learn, especially if you think, as when choosing clothes, in terms of blocks of colour and unified schemes. The key to the successful planning of whole houses or apartments is to think in terms of easy flow.

When it comes to deciding upon colours for a room, light is the most important factor. You should also think about the views through the windows, which you will sometimes want to emphasize and sometimes fade out. Some rooms which are not blessed with flooding daylight can be made to *look* more cheerful by making the floor as light as possible and by using light and airy colours (off-whites, whites, creams, yellows, greens and accents of rose) to take advantage of garden, landscape or other views from the windows. Others, which are dark because there are buildings or heavy trees too close to the windows, will look much better, warmer and cosier, if there is no

pretence that they could ever look light and airy; here you should rely on rich colouring, bright accents and clever lighting.

Of course you might have set your heart upon a blue and white room, or a mainly yellow, red or green room. But if you feel uninspired about colour schemes, don't despair; very few people start entirely from scratch in a home. You will almost certainly possess some sort of item you will *have* to use. It might be a rug, a painting, a set of prints, a sofa or an armchair you do not need, or cannot afford, to have re-covered. This is what you should use as the starting point for your selection of a colour scheme. What is the main colour, or colours, of the piece? This colour, or combination of colours, can serve as your base, from which you can build up accent and contrast colours.

Selecting Colour

✔ When asked how to select colours, I invariably suggest the same solution as with the question of styles. This is to go and buy as many decorating magazines and books as possible and go through them, marking pages in books and cutting out magazine photographs of rooms that seem particularly appealing. Put them aside for a week or so and then go through them again. Sifting through your choices later, you will almost certainly find that much of the colouring is the same. This should give you a clear idea of the colours which instinctively appeal to you.

✔ When you have got together samples of possible wall, floor and window coverings, tablecloths, upholstery, pillows and so on, put them all down on a table in the room in which you are going to use them (both in daylight and in artificial light). Stare long and hard at them with narrowed eyes. By having a good squint at all those assembled colours, textures and patterns, you will quickly see which ones work well together, in what proportions, and which stand out as being obviously wrong.

TOP: Pale terracotta floor tiles and the faded roses and greens of the Oriental rug set the colour scheme in this French room. All the rest — curtains, cloth and chair colours — follow suit.

ABOVE: A purple armchair is balanced by a rose and purple rug and similarly coloured glass and ceramics. The colours stand out with jewel-like clarity in the otherwise white room. .

UNDERSTANDING LIGHT

Artificial light is certainly the most flexible way to change the mood, atmosphere or feeling of a room. You can exaggerate space or diminish faults at the flick of a switch or the turn of a dimmer. Unconsidered lighting can make an otherwise impeccable room look dreary, whereas imaginative lighting can imbue the simplest space with a special quality.

There have been enormous advances in domestic lighting over the last two decades or so, but many people still think of lighting in connection with the actual fixtures, rather than as a medium that can be manipulated like paint. When they buy lights or lamps, they all too often buy them just for their shapes and looks, rather than for their effect. Even when searching out the more sophisticated lighting in a shop or catalogue – spots, wall-washers, downlights, uplights and floor-standing halogen lights – they go mostly for looks without finding out what those looks will achieve.

ABOVE: Daylight filtering through the windows streaks and dapples this porch-surrounded Australian room. At night, similar pools and patches of light can be created by lamps and uplights strategically placed on side tables, behind pieces of furniture or in corners.

LIGHTING ANGLES (BELOW, LEFT TO RIGHT): An adjustable spotlight, a table lamp, a floor lamp, an eliptical wall light, an adjustable reading light, a pendant light and a concealed strip light.

It *is* difficult to display the effects of lighting, particularly of the wide new variety of bulbs, anywhere except in a showroom devoted to nothing else. In a small area, full of different fixtures crammed together for maximum choice, it is virtually impossible to show how the position, colour and intensity of light sources will give definition to various spaces in a home.

Whenever possible, therefore, it is wise to visit proper lighting showrooms (which are, like all designer showrooms in this economic climate, now much easier to get into without a designer). This is generally the best and most efficient way to get an accurate view of current techniques. If it is not possible to do this, take careful note of pleasing lighting in other people's homes and in restaurants, museums and galleries – anywhere and anything that it seems possible to translate into a domestic setting. If you make a conscious effort to find out how a particular effect is achieved you will be well on your way to better lighting plans.

TYPES OF LIGHT

Each room needs three kinds of light:

• Background (or ambient) light to provide general cover across the room as a whole.

• Work (or task) light to read or work by.

• Accent light to highlight plants, flowers, art, sculpture – anything you particularly would like to draw attention to.

There is also a fourth group which one might term atmospheric light. This is the most romantic but the least effective for seeing by and is provided by candlelight, oil light and firelight.

The best sort of background (or ambient) light is the reflective variety – that is, light that bounces off a wall – because it produces the least glare. This can be obtained from a number of sources. It can come indirectly, for example from more or less concealed uplights placed in corners, behind plants and behind furniture; from light concealed behind bays, wooden valances, or plaster cornices; from wallwashers of one kind or another (which literally 'wash' the walls with light if mounted on or recessed into the ceiling some 45 to 90 cm (18 in to 3 ft) from the wall); from wall lights casting light up or down, or both, depending upon the fixture; and finally, from direct lighting like table lamps or floor lamps. The tungsten halogen variety with their own built-in dimmers are particularly effective for this purpose because they are capable of such a punch that they can light up a whole room on their own.

Whatever you choose, try not to let general light be all one level of brightness. Our eyes see by means of contrast, and nothing makes a room seem as flat and boring as the bland light given by a lone central ceiling fitting – the only exception to this being if you can fit one of the new and interestingly designed varieties with diffusing elements set into an opaque shade which give a much more varied kind of light. If possible, always try to install dimmer switches for all lighting fixtures, including uplights, for you will then be able to control their intensity at the touch of a finger.

Work or task light requires a different set of rules. The job of this type of lighting is not only to allow us to see what we are doing without strain, but also to give the best sort of light for specific work. Writing letters, drawing, reading, typing, working at a computer, chopping

Bulb Types

✔ Over the last few years there has been an enormous increase in the types of bulbs produced for the domestic market. They now come in all shapes and sizes and are designed for many different uses. Tungsten filament bulbs are still the most widely bought, but tungsten halogen, linear fluorescent and the newish mini-fluorescent bulbs are now becoming much more popular.

✔ Tungsten filament bulbs are available with pearlized, clear or coloured glass. Some have silvered fronts to direct light down on to a reflector; some are internally silvered reflector bulbs. They are available from 15 to 150 watts, and are made in a variety of shapes (mushroom, candle, golfball and strip, as well as the standard shape). Many US bulbs are three-way for different intensities.

✔ Low-voltage tungsten halogen bulbs are tiny (you should never touch them with bare fingers when screwing them in, or they will be ruined). They give a brilliant burst of light and range from 20 to 100 watts. They have the advantage, however, of not giving off as much heat as a conventional bulb. Their shapes range from those looking like miniature jam-jars to slim, linear strips and narrow tubes doubled back into a hairpin shape. They are also available in higher wattages for external fittings.

(See also p. 138)

vegetables, making a sauce, sewing, all require special lighting to provide a localized area of brighter light than the general level of light throughout the room. The light should fall on whatever task we are doing without casting shadows or causing glare, so positioning is also critical. For example, a right-handed person will need a desk lamp to be placed to the left to prevent the writer's arm from causing a shadow, and vice versa. Light fixtures should be a reasonable distance behind anyone reading, so that light falls over a right or left shoulder; if the light source is from a downlight overhead, it should fall a foot in front of the work or book, otherwise the illumination will be too bright.

In fact, reading does not require as much light as most of us would expect, because the degree of contrast between print and page helps legibility. Most 60-year-olds, however, need more light than a 30-year-old, and if you are spending, say, five hours on a project in an office, you will need more light than you would for a half-hour session. Another point to remember is that it is important to strike a nice balance between the work surface and its surroundings: the surroundings should be no less than one third the brightness of the work surface, or you certainly will get eye strain.

Kitchen tasks are well served by fluorescent lights concealed behind a board or valance above the working surface. Circular or miniature fluorescent tubes are good for tasks concentrated on a smaller area, as

are tungsten halogen which are excellent when a really high level of illumination is called for. The latter are much better than high-wattage tungsten filament bulbs which are bulky and tend to overheat fittings.

Far too many bedside lights are placed too low for reading comfortably. As I have stressed, light should fall on to a book from over the shoulder, not from under it. Almost certainly the best reading light for beds – and, for that matter, sofas set against a wall – are swing-arm wall lamps with integral dimmers fixed at the most appropriate height for you.

Manipulating accent light for pictures, objects or textures is quite an art in itself, as getting the right amount of light and the correct positioning is crucial. When you are successful, however, the balance of light and shade, glow and drama, that you can infuse into a room can be spectacular.

WALL LIGHTING

When you want to throw a wash of light over a chosen wall you can

position and angle a row of lights – wallwashers or angled downlights – to illuminate either the whole wall or a part of it. It is an excellent method for lighting a collection of closely hung prints or drawings, or a wall full of books, and can be used in such a way that the available space seems to expand. Another type of lighting called wall grazing uses slightly stronger, more acutely angled light to pick out interesting textures such as brick, old panelling, a tapestry or wall hanging. Neither method should be used if the wall is very shiny or lacquered, or if there are irregularities in the surface that you do not want shown off.

In either event, recessed lights should, if possible, be installed at least 45 cm (18 in) from the wall (as I have already mentioned for wall washing), and somewhat closer, say 22 to 30 cm (9 to 12 in) for wall grazing. If it is difficult to recess lights, then use track-mounted versions. What is critical, however, is the distance lights are placed apart from one another. If the gaps are too wide, the lights will tend to produce

43

LEFT: Small, carefully positioned table lamps provide accent light for the collection of objects as well as lighting up the wine rack in this French hallway.

RIGHT: The fanciful tall lamp beside the (equally fanciful) bed is well positioned for bedtime reading.

a distinct scalloped effect along the top of the wall. You may, of course, like this look, which can be decorative in its own right, but if you do not, find out the exact spread of light that you require and buy only those lamps that give the widest possible beam. The best bulbs to use for grazing are tungsten reflectors because standard bulbs produce too diffuse a light. Be aware, too, that the higher the wattage of the bulb, the more pronounced the effect; you will certainly need brighter bulbs if walls are dark.

Another method for wall grazing is to fix a row of bare, silvered spotlights behind a wooden valance or fascia board, painted matt white on the inside for better reflection.

LIGHTING PICTURES

Groups of pictures on a wall, as has already been mentioned, can be excellently lit by wallwashers. If, however, recessed or track light, or even fluorescent strips concealed behind a cover or fascia board, are not practical or desirable, you could achieve a reasonable effect with a row of small portable adjustable uplights, which can be appropriately angled from the floor.

Individual paintings, on the other hand, are notoriously difficult to light really well. Here are some pointers:

• Do not hang paintings on walls with windows because daylight glare will prevent you from seeing them properly.

• Do not position tungsten or incandescent light fixtures too near to works of art (especially those on paper) because they can cause heat damage.

• All light can cause colours to fade, particularly watercolours, which should be exposed only to the lowest possible light levels. Whatever the bulb type used (fluorescent light is generally preferable for such

objects), an ultra-violet (UV) filter should also be used to minimize harmful rays.

• If oil paintings are very glossy, or if glass over a picture reflects light, the best solution is to reposition light fixtures. Usually an angle of between 40° to 60° to the perpendicular will cut down glare. If it does not, try a 70° angle, or move the picture down very slightly towards the floor. Non-reflective glass can work well over watercolours, prints, posters, photographs and textiles, but is less successful over oils.

• If you are going to use classic picture lights with a brass or silver finish, these are usually mounted right on, or just above, the frame. They can be angled to avoid glare, but do remember that, in order to light the whole picture, the fitting should measure at least two-thirds the width of the frame.

• If you decide that spotlights are more discreet, remember that the angle, as stated above, is most important. Spots or mini-spots can be recessed into the ceiling, hung on a track or, less neatly, surface-mounted. The best bulb to use is a low-voltage tungsten halogen variety, but, unfortunately, even the most careful positioning can result in an overspill of light. You can avoid this problem by using the expensive framing projectors which can focus the light so as exactly to encompass any shape or object.

LIGHTING FEATURES

If there are architectural features that you especially want to light up, it is wise to bear in mind that too much light directed at a certain point can flatten rather than delineate. It is therefore preferable to light them obliquely with tiny halogen spots, anchored as inconspicuously as possible, rather than to subject them to a full-frontal assault. To emphasize a texture, for instance

the unevenness of a wall in an old house, uplights placed on the floor below are usually found to be the best solution.

ATMOSPHERIC LIGHTING

Romantic lighting of any sort is undoubtedly best achieved with candlelight and/or firelight and, perhaps, very discreetly dimmed background light coming from judiciously placed uplights concealed in corners, behind furniture and underneath plants. Pink bulbs, of course, will warm up any lamp and make its light a good deal more flattering, just as blue or green bulbs will make rooms look more shady in hot weather. Remember, too, that filters and gels are available in all sorts of colours from lighting stores, and can be fitted over the tops of bulbs to change completely the mood and feeling of a room. Red gels, for example, will make a room cosy, warm and glowing; green – dark and mysterious; blue – creepily ghostly.

CHRISTMAS AND HOLIDAY LIGHTING

Strings of plain Christmas-tree lights can be used to great effect in places other than on the tree itself. They look marvellous at Christmas and on other winter holiday occasions, hung around the branches of large plants, across windows, amongst foliage, intertwined with wreaths, tightly strung under cornices or applied to ceiling moulding. Remember to check them regularly and ensure that they are turned off periodically.

SPECIAL REQUIREMENTS

In addition to work, accent and mood light, you will need special kinds of lighting for daily tasks such as making-up and shaving. The best light for making-up is shed from the sides of a mirror; the best for shaving from above. In both cases, this is most effective with theatrical strips; these should be fixed around three sides of the mirror, ideally with separate switches for top and sides, since most home-owners use bathroom mirrors for both functions. If at all possible, attach a dimmer switch, for the lights can become glaringly hot. If you cannot place light on all three sides, a light immediately above the mirror is the next best thing. And if theatrical strips are not available, but side light is still possible, use swing-arm lamps positioned to shine outwards rather than on the mirror.

Children's rooms, too, require special light. Wall lights, although expensive and difficult to install, are useful as they will give a softer, more diffused light than central ceiling fixtures; but do try to install a dimmer switch. Very low wattage skirting or base board fixtures are also excellent for children who are afraid of sleeping alone in the dark. Older children, of course, will need good light for homework, hobbies, games and for reading in bed; outlets should be provided by work surfaces and beds, as trailing wires are a safety hazard.

A wall light provides ambient light in this kitchen, while strip lights and spots serve the hob and shelves. Note the decorative strings of fairy lights fixed around both sides of the louvred blind forming the countertop divider.

Lighting Safety and Security

✔ Make sure that all outlets in children's bedrooms, or in any other rooms that they frequent, are childproofed and shuttered. All electrical appliances should be kept well out of reach.

✔ If there are children, elderly or short-sighted people in a household, it is a good idea to have dim corridor and stair lights on during the night to reduce the likelihood of accidents. Always light up unexpected steps down, or changes of level, with skirting or base board, low-wattage fixtures. It is, of course, extremely important to make sure that the treads of stairs are well lit, not just by night, but, if daylight is scarce in the stairwell area, by day as well.

✔ Make sure that any approaches to houses are properly-lit, and that there is adequate light above front and back doors to see to open them by.

✔ If houses or apartments are often empty, it is certainly a good idea to get a timing device which puts lights on and off and switches radios or television on at irregular intervals.

45

TEXTURE AND PATTERN

At the beginning of this chapter I talked about how colours are radically altered by different textures and patterns. In fact, variations and tones in a single colour can make a monochromatic scheme as lively and effective as a room with dramatically contrasting colour. Take white, for example. Try to imagine the varying degrees and depths of white that you find in the following: white voile, silk, marble, corduroy, velvet, damask, paint, tweed, tile, leather, sailcloth, wicker, and white sheepskin rugs. Go through the same process with a different colour. This simple but pleasing exercise should give you a notion of the sort of contrasts and variants you can achieve simply by using the different textures within a monochromatic scheme.

Clearly, some textures are better juxtaposed than others, just as some colours are better used together than others. It is obvious that rough is at the opposite end of the scale from smooth, and shiny at the opposite end from matt. The extent to which you will wish to combine

them, however, is a matter of taste and instinct. If you feel unconfident, all you have to do is try to collect as many different examples of different textures of the same colour and juggle them around until you discover juxtapositions that please you. It is worth remembering that, although it can be jarring and unrestful to have too many colours in a room, there is almost no limit to the number of textures that can be introduced.

Contrasting and mixing textures, however, is a breeze compared to mixing patterns, an exercise in decoration which considerably frightens a good many people.

In the eighteenth and early nineteenth centuries, when patterned fabrics started to become widely available to the middle as well as to the upper classes, the norm was to keep rooms all of a piece, with window and bed treatments, walls and furnishings harmonizing in scale and colour. In Victorian times there was a greater choice of patterns and, because of the invention of new dyes, of colours. But although the number of pieces of furniture and accessories ran riot, the use of pat-

terns was still fairly restrained. The modern movements of the early twentieth century reacted against pattern, tending to favour large expanses of flat colour. It has only been in the last part of the twentieth century, as the choice of designs has become increasingly wider, that pattern has been given free rein. So much so that sometimes you can go into a room and be forgiven for thinking that the owners were trying to win a bizarre competition for pattern collecting.

Thankfully, a great many fabric and wallpaper manufacturers, aware of the pitfalls, have tried to make matters easier by grouping together co-ordinating designs so that it is difficult for customers to make a mistake. But this too has its drawbacks; the comprehensive suggestions made by the more popular manufacturers result in many homes acquiring a kind of uniform, whereas it is obviously preferable for interiors to look as individual and personal as possible.

So what is the trick to mixing patterns confidently and with skill? Again, it is really a question of training the eye. As usual, one way

46

Pattern-Collating Tips

In these four distinctive rooms patterns of all different types and scales – including stripes, checks and florals – combine with ease. This is largely due to the fact that each has a strong unifying colour scheme.

of doing this is to analyse the number, the use and differing proportions of patterns in rooms, or photographs or paintings of rooms that you like. The patterns in the rooms that please you are likely to be generally the same in colouring and tone, with fairly gentle contrasts of scale or proportion.

A mix of pattern that is easy on the eye will probably consist of one fairly large-scale design contrasted with a geometric pattern – a stripe, plaid or check, trellis or even polka dots – and probably some smaller all-over floral, leaf or fishscale design with some connection to the larger pattern. Again, there might be some thematic connection such as differing leaves against white or cream backgrounds used with a stripe or check. Most importantly, the patterns will almost certainly have a common denominator in colouring, if not in theme as well.

✔ Generally it is best not to use more than one large-scale design in a room (or two at the most, as long as they are similar in scale, colour and feeling). You can, however, use several different small-scale patterns in conjunction with a larger design. A larger pattern on a window treatment and/or walls gives a good sense of perspective if used with smaller patterns on blinds, upholstery, pillows or cushions. You could also line larger-patterned curtains or draperies with a smaller-scale pattern, or the same pattern, perhaps in a contrast colourway.

✔ Similar designs in the same colours usually combine quite happily, as when patterned window treatments, rugs or carpets are complemented by smaller-scale patterns. A similar design in two different colours can also look good, as can the same pattern reversed (or in negative), for example, blue on white, with white on blue.

✔ An exception to the rule of not using too many patterns together can be made with patterns of the same feeling and colouring. For instance, a variety of paisleys, Indian fabrics or batiks can be used in addition to Oriental rugs, and small Liberty or other prints can easily be mixed with other similar nineteenth-century designs.

✔ Do not forget the subtle effect of using sheers printed with the same main design as the over-curtains. This can be equally effective with an allied design, or a smaller-scale design using the same motif. The print can be in one colour on white, white on white, or in a paler version of the colour of the over-curtains.

✔ You can take advantage of the manufacturers' skilful collations of patterns and co-ordinates in fabrics and wallpapers and still add your own touches. These might be, for example, old needlework pillows or cushions, objects that you have embroidered yourself, old shawls, throws or blankets, rugs and old quilts, all subtly blending with the colouring or feeling of the fabrics and/or paper. Moreover, if you make a habit of studying the way these mass-market collections are put together, you will soon be able to form your own groupings from different sources, mixing old with new, the conventional with the idiosyncratic.

✔ However many rulings and possibilities you hear about in the abstract, nothing quite compares with experience. So once again, take the trouble to collect together as many samples of fabrics and wallpapers as you can. Play around with them, look at them together with your current possessions and decoration, and in different lights, and see what seems to go best together, before putting them into various groupings. Very soon you will build up as much confidence with texture and pattern mixing, as you should have by now with colours.

47

THE BASIC
room

O nce you have more or less settled on the style, lighting, colours and form for your room, or rooms – and, of course, the extent of your budget – it is time to focus on the walls, ceilings, floors, windows and general furnishings. These are the basic components, or bare bones, of a room, and only once you have decided how they are to be treated should you go on to choose accessories and add the finishing touches. It is best to evolve a plan that can be achieved in stages, so that, even if your budget is going to be very small to start with, you can establish priorities along the way. By exercising a little ingenuity, there should be no need to feel pressured to spend more than you can afford: remember that having more dash than cash has never hurt anyone.

I purposely began this chapter using the words 'more or less' because it is important to remember that decorating with any pretension to comfort and warmth is in no way an exact science. There are far too many unpredictables in even the best laid plans for things always to proceed smoothly. Fabrics, wall and floor coverings, light fixtures, paint colours and pieces of furniture that you may have set your heart upon can all turn out to be frustratingly elusive, horribly expensive or simply unavailable

LEFT: Subtle paintwork and voile curtains make an inexpensive but effective background.
RIGHT: Cool, reflective surfaces bind disparate objects and various decorative elements in these rooms.

Equally, as I have frequently mentioned before, accident or chance can also play its part, and you may well end up with a look that you might have not previously envisaged. Decorating is more about the spirit of enterprise and the art of compromise than precise planning.

As in most things, an open mind can overcome the frustration inherent in decorating, and even the most tedious happenings can sometimes be turned to good advantage. Always remember that you do not *have* to plunge in to a new and expensive decorating scheme straight away and that there are usually many alternatives.

GOOD COMPROMISES

The initial effort of buying a home, or even the down payment of rent, can mean that there is little left over for decoration. There is always room, however, for compromise – at least at first. Walls, ceilings and woodwork can get by for some time with a fresh coat of paint, or you can hang really cheap fabric such as

cheesecloth from the ceiling to the floor. Walls which are damaged (provided they are not damp) can be temporarily supported with a tough lining paper and wallpaper.

Wood floors which are in reasonable condition can be stripped, sanded and polished; they can also be stained or bleached and then polished. For further floor decoration, you can always add a stencilled border, a painted rug, a floor cloth or conventional rug, or even an interesting wallpaper border.

Old wood floors that are in danger of wearing if given one more sanding (a layer or two of wood is stripped off each time), can be miraculously restored with a coat of primer and a top coat of paint. This can be left plain, stencilled or overpainted with a design of some sort. But whatever treatment you choose should be sealed with at least two coats of clear polyurethane, leaving twenty-four hours' drying time between coats. Probably the best way to apply the polyurethane is with a roller, brushing out any

small air bubbles that appear. Although it may appear tedious to have to wait so long between coats, the end result is well worth it, because the layered varnish will make the floor as hard as tiles and as easy to clean.

Worn or stained carpeting can be dyed a darker colour; and, like wood, old linoleum or vinyl tiles can be painted and sealed, or covered with squares of hardboard (masonite), then painted in two colours and 'marbled'. Windows do not have to have expensive curtains and can look very good with alternative treatments such as shelves, screens or a variety of hanging plants. You can certainly get away for quite some time with odds and ends of furnishings and with the minimum of furniture, provided that your first expenditure is on a comfortable bed and sofa. What follows are some useful summaries of the choices available for the different components of your rooms once you feel that you are able to embark upon them.

ABOVE: Stencilled panels, marbled dado and stained floor, lend distinction .
LEFT: A stripped floor, rag-rolled walls and angled shelves add interest and detail.

WALLS

Given their area, walls have an important visual role to play in the decoration of a room, quite apart from their framing and protective qualities. So how you choose to treat them – in terms of colour and finish (whether paint, paper, fabric or panelling) – will, of course, affect the overall character of the room.

PROPORTIONS AND DETAILS

Even before making these important decisions, however, you should think about the proportions of your walls and whether they can be improved upon. Consider also whether any existing details, such as cornices, crown mouldings, picture rails, chair rails, skirting (or base boards), mantlepieces, window types, doors and door-cases, are appropriate and whether, if they do not exist, they should be added.

In the post-World War II years much handsome detailing was torn out of old buildings in an attempt to make rooms look more modern; only comparatively recently have mouldings begun to be added to new buildings as a matter of course.

Ceilings that are too high for the length and width of the walls can be made to seem lower by being painted a slightly darker shade than the walls – a rather more subtle approach than painting them a different darker colour. You can also make the walls seem better proportioned and more distinguished by adding a crown moulding or cornice at the conjunction of ceiling and walls. If a shallow moulding already exists you could deepen it by pasting up a wallpaper border or part of a paper border (see wallpapers, p. 55) just below it. Adding a chair rail or dado, more or less at waist height, is also effective. Underneath it you can then use contrasting or deeper coloured paint, a differently patterned or coloured wallpaper or real, or *faux* (false) panelling. Skirting boards can be made to look more important by the addition of some extra moulding or, again, part of a wallpaper border: whole borders can look too heavy.

All sorts of mouldings – from cornices, dados and pediments to pilasters and arches – are widely available now in light and inexpensive polystyrene. They are easy to stick up and, with a coat of paint, make an instant and apparently magical change in the look of a room – even if they cannot quite compare with genuine plaster and carved wood mouldings.

Wallpaper borders, whether used with wallpaper or plain paint, are an alternative decorative feature and can serve to delineate the space very neatly in a variety of ways. For example, a whole border can be pasted up just under the ceiling, and the border of that border cut off and pasted round door and window frames, above or below the dado (or used instead of a dado if none exists) as well as above the skirting boards. Again, a narrow border can be used for the corners of a room, or to simulate panelling – with a paint shade or wallpaper which is different from the surrounding walls inside the 'panel'.

Ceilings that are too low look less oppressive if painted a lighter colour than the walls. More ambitiously, you can add some *trompe l'oeil* ('fool the eye') effect, either with paint or paper architectural borders, to form an apparent tray or raised ceiling, or even a dome or sky effect.

SPECIAL PAINT EFFECTS

Trompe l'oeil, faux paint finishes and other illusionist techniques are, of course, nothing new. They were widely used by the ancient Egyptians, Greeks and Romans and have been popular ever since. During the Renaissance in Italy in the fifteenth century, especially beautiful and complicated paint finishes were executed. Only in the wake of the modernist strictures of the Bauhaus School in the first quarter of the twentieth century did such decorative finishes go out of favour.

In the last decade or so, however, people have once again discovered the traditional skills of painted decoration. With the vast range of sophisticated paint types, colours and shades available, as well as ready-mixed glazes (see p. 53) and brushes, the patient and painstaking amateur can now produce very impressive finishes.

DRAGGING OR STRIÉ This is the technique of dragging a wide, *dry* brush (graining tool or broom) through a tinted, usually darker, transparent glaze coat applied over a lighter, opaque base. It takes a bit of practice, and you will need two people working at once on the job: one to roll on the glaze over the dry base

51

PAINT EFFECTS

DRAGGING: The 'dragging' technique – whatever the favoured tool – provides a pleasant irregular surface, especially suitable for breaking up large blocks and areas of plain colour.

STIPPLING: 'Stippled' finishes – looking rather like the skin of an orange – are particularly useful for smallish areas like door and window frames, chair rails and raised panelling.

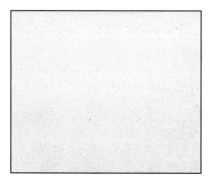

SPONGING: 'Sponging' – achieved exactly as it sounds by dabbing at wet glaze with an ordinary household sponge – gives a nice soft finish to a wall as well as to large pieces of furniture.

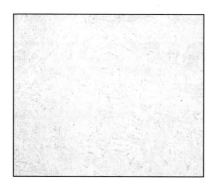

RAGGING: Like sponging, 'ragging' makes for a soft wall finish, and can be achieved not just with a bunched-up rag but with hessian, tissue, lace or even a plastic bag.

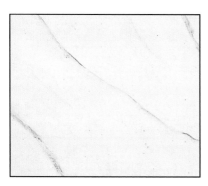

MARBLING: Professional-looking marble finish is surprising easy to reproduce, but do have a good sample or photograph of the real thing to copy. You can use the technique for cheering up mantlepieces, skirting or base boards, or floors.

STENCILLING: The ancient techniques of stencilling can be used to decorate floors, walls and furniture, as well as fabrics, so long as the surface is not too shiny. Use your own or pre-cut stencils.

ABOVE: In this colourfully exotic entrance hall walls are sponged and doors are dragged and stippled with *faux* Middle-Eastern panels. The fancifully painted chair and highly patterned kelim complete the effect.

LEFT: This *trompe l'oeil* is painted on canvas by American painter, Kathie Noonan Lang, and stuck over a partition wall . Shelves are exactly aligned with the real shelves on either side and are topped by a pediment made from white-painted lengths of moulding.

coat, the other to follow quickly behind with the glazing tool. Special dragging brushes called 'floggers' are expensive and generally come rather wide. But if you are only going to do a one-off job, it makes more sense to buy an ordinary but good quality 12 cm (5 in) brush; you will, however, have to work more quickly because the brush will cover less ground at a time. Cheap brushes which shed their bristles are a false economy. Equally, you can improvise with other graining tools such as an afro or toothed comb.

Once you have tested your glaze on a board, start the glazing and dragging procedure from a corner of the room so you will have a guiding vertical line to follow. As one person uses a brush or roller to apply the glaze in strips, not allowing one band to dry before the next is brushed on, the partner should quickly drag the dry brush down through the glaze with a light but steady pressure. Wipe the brush or tool with a rag as soon as the dragged-off glaze begins to accumulate, or you will find you are putting more back than you take off.

STIPPLING This is simpler than dragging, but still requires two people. The orange-peel texture is produced by the glaze bring dabbed rather than dragged off. Any brush with a broad, blunt cut will do, but, again, it should be wiped frequently.

Another method of stippling involves wads of scrumpled-up rags or wax paper with which to dab off the glaze. Wads like this work faster than brushes and can be chucked away when full of glaze. A long-napped roller is also somewhat faster than a brush.

SPONGING This is very similar to stippling, except that the chosen tool is a large sponge which is again dabbed or 'pounced' on to the glaze.

Glazing Tips

✔ The most frequently used decorative finishes are all based on different handlings of glaze. Commercial glaze has the consistency of cream of chicken soup but provides a transparent film, usually tinted and applied over an opaque base. Tinted glazes are either 'distressed' (with broken colour, according to the paint finish of choice) or built up in various coats to provide a lovely translucent effect.

✔ Glazes can be tinted with 'universal tinters', or ordinary artists' oil paints if you want more esoteric shades. Using different colour groups for the tinted glaze and the base coat can produce quite different and translucent colours which are superior to any commercial shade.. If the glaze is tinted with a hue in the same family as the base coat, the result will be a deepened tone of that base colour.

✔ On the whole, you will need much less glaze than paint to cover the walls. Usually glaze is thinned somewhat with mineral or white spirits, but be aware that these make it dry more rapidly, so you will have to work more quickly.

✔ Try out all *faux* finishes on sample boards, suitably primed, before you start on the walls. Once you have successfully applied a particular technique to your walls, protect the newly decorated surface with a couple of coats of polyurethane.

✔ Most polyurethanes have a slightly yellowing, darkening effect on paint. This can give a mellow, antiqued effect, but if you want your colours to be fresh and pellucid, ask in hardware stores for non-yellowing polyurethanes.

53

RAGGING A more haphazard and ragged version of rag-stippling, this can be done by one person alone. Bunched-up rags that have been moistened in turpentine or mineral spirits are used with a circular motion of the wrist, alternating the pressure and the direction to vary the texture. Lightly wadded cheese-cloth, burlap or tissue paper creates a sharpened texture, which looks good on woodwork. Plastic rubbish bags give a nice soft, blurry effect.

LACQUERING Genuine lacquering is extremely time-consuming, but you can achieve several lacquer-like effects by gradually building up coats of either tinted polyurethane varnish or tinted glaze over your chosen base of paint colour. Remember, however, that high gloss lacquer can draw attention to less than perfect walls.

MARBLING There are as many ways to 'marblize' as there are types of marble. For that cloudy, veined effect you need to practise your technique on a board first, using a darker tinted glaze or a 'drifty', random pattern over the base coat. The mottled effect is achieved by dabbing the surface of the glaze with a rag or sponge dipped in mineral spirits to soften the edges.

The marble's veins can be painted on, ideally with a goose or turkey feather or a small brush. The colour can be made up in stronger tones of glaze – either in the marble's basic colour or in altogether different colours.

STENCILLING Commercially pre-cut stencil kits are widely available in any number of designs. But, as long

LEFT: Blue and white stencils adapted from the design of the rug create extremely effective door and window surrounds as well as a dado in this room.

as you keep the designs very simple, you can also make your own stencils.

Once you are happy with the design – you can blow up or reduce the scale in a photocopier – trace it out, remembering to isolate the various parts of the design as cut-outs. Then colour the different parts on the tracing paper with crayons. You can always experiment with alternative colourways on a fresh piece of tracing paper.

Trace the design on to a sheet of acetate. Next, cut out the stencil, turning the design as you cut. Mix your paint rather thickly so that it does not run underneath the edges of the stencil. Now tape the stencil to the wall with masking tape.

Dip a small piece of sponge into one of the paint colours, removing any excess paint. Then dab the sponge through the appropriate part of the stencil on to the wall, working one opening at a time. You may find it easier to work on the thinner sections, such as stems, with a small brush. When you have filled in all the cut-out areas, untape the acetate and lift it straight up to avoid smudging the paint, before starting on the next section. Again any special detailing can be done with a brush.

The final touch is to give the wall a coat of polyurethane. This allows you to wash the wall and preserve the stencilling.

WALLPAPERS

Wallpapers can add distinction and interest to less than perfect rooms as well as disguise rough or uneven walls. In fact, thanks to a break-through that is the equivalent of the zip for clothes, it is now even possible to paper over brick or concrete walls with success.

For a large part of the twentieth century, wallpaper has been out of fashion. Now it is back in vogue

with an almost limitless choice of papers. There are machine-made papers, hand-blocked papers, metallics, flocks, textured papers, washable vinyls and many others offering a host of designs, old and new, at both ends of the market.

Cheap papers can be made to look more distinctive and last longer with a coat of polyurethane. Expensive papers can be made to go further by using them only below or above a chair rail. Another saving is to cut the paper up into panels and edge it with narrow wooden mouldings, lengths of picture framing or strips of paper border.

Wallpaper borders are also making a popular comeback on both sides of the Atlantic, with an enormous range to choose from. They can be used to finish off co-ordinating or *faux* finish papers and to give definition to a painted wall or the inside of a ceiling. For narrow edgings try cutting off strips and using them around doors and window frames, down the corners of walls, or wherever standard-sized borders might look too wide and clumsy.

One of the cheaper ways of adding instant elegance to a room is to use some of the cut-out paper architectural motifs available – elaborate swags and cornices, pilasters, chair rails and panelled or pictorial dados. You can also create your own borders by cutting into strips any wallpaper with the right sort of lineal design: for example, side-by-side vertical repeats or stripes that can be cut and used horizontally.

ALTERNATIVE WALLCOVERINGS

As well as the many paint and paper effects you can create, you can make walls look handsome and luxurious by covering them in various fabrics. Two comparatively easy ways of achieving this are shirring and stapling.

55

SHIRRING Generously shirring (or gathering) light, cheap fabrics such as cheesecloth, voile, tight-weave muslin and sheeting cotton is a very effective, and inexpensive, short-term solution for walls. Not only can it be unthreaded and laundered within a day, provided it is machine washable, but it is also easy to do.

You will need about three times each wall's width of fabric, as well as slim rods of wooden dowels to be mounted all around the room just below the ceiling and above the skirting boards; gaps above doors, windows and mantlepieces should have small lengths of rod above the frames. Hem the fabric top and bottom so that the rods of dowels can be threaded through, and then push the fabric up to form gathers. You can also hang lengths of fabric like curtains by simply mounting rods all around the room just under the ceiling. The fabric can then be threaded through the rods and allowed to hang loose, either just touching or breaking on to the floor. It can be drawn back on either side of windows and mantlepieces and to one side of doors.

STAPLING Any fabric with a fairly tight weave (that won't stretch, buckle or wrinkle) can be stapled on to walls as an easy cover-up. Cut panels of the fabric to the length of your walls, and seam them together either by sewing them in the conventional way, or by overlapping and stapling them. (Do not glue butted or overlapping panels: the glue can discolour and harden the fabric.) Staple the fabric to the walls about every 7.5 cm (3 in) along the top and bottom of each panel. Always begin stapling at the top, smoothing, not stretching, the fabric until you get to a corner. Staple down the side, and then along the bottom, giving the fabric gentle tugs as you go along to keep it taut and smooth.

The professional method of upholstering walls (called 'walling') is expensive. First the walls are lined with a soft, padded lining material (known as a 'bump'). Then the seamed material is attached to slim wooden battens fixed to the walls laterally below the ceiling or cornice and above the skirting board, and vertically at regular intervals. But even with amateur stapling, you can approximate to this padded look by lining the walls with panels of lining material cut to the exact size of your top panels. Staple marks can be hidden by a trim, for example, lengths of decorative picture framing, ribbon, gimp, or even slim rolls of the fabric itself.

WOOD PANELLING All sorts of wood panelling are available, and there are various methods of treating it. These range from distressing it to covering it with high gloss paint. However, unless you are a skilled carpenter, it is best to get professional help with any installation.

FLOORS

Floors need careful consideration. They have to withstand a tougher beating than any other surface in a home and will inevitably take a sizable chunk of your budget. You will have to consider how to make them fit in with your decorating plans and how best to maintain them. It may be worth considering the most practical and economical options before planning any expensive floor treatments.

SOFT FLOORS

There was a time when the choice of 'soft' floor carpeting was comparatively simple: you bought Axminster, Brussels weave, Wilton, wool cord, twist Berber, shag pile or carpet tiles in either pure wool, wool and nylon or nylon or acrylic

BELOW: The marbled black-and-white diamond floor looks both fresh and elegant in this spacious yellow-painted hallway.

and in standard widths: either body carpeting (less than 1.8 m or 6 ft) or broadloom (1.8 m or 6 ft; 2.75 m or 9 ft; 3.7 m or 12 ft). Now, however, there is such a profusion of different types of fibre and terms to describe them that it is worth printing a vocabulary with a note on what goes best where.

There are some general points, however, which are worth noting. Short pile, dense carpets tend to wear much better than longer pile varieties. Most carpets have either a woven or a foam backing; in woven carpets the pile and backing are woven together, while in the tufted variety, fibres are inserted individually into a specially treated backing which is then sealed with an adhesive to hold them firmly in place. In some carpets, the fibres are electrostatically flocked to the backing. Woven carpets need to be laid by a professional using underlay; non-woven carpets can be laid by the amateur. Carpet tiles can either be loose-laid or stuck down.

Matting, whether sisal, coir, grassweave or rush, makes an excellent neutral flooring. It is particularly good at uniting a disparate or eclectic selection of furniture. What it lacks in softness and luxury, it more than makes up for in crisp textural contrast. Matting now also comes in a whole range of natural colours and weaves, from basketweave to herringbone and simpler textures; it also takes dyes well and is now often painted with designs as well.

HARD FLOORS

Although the choice here is greater, paradoxically 'hard' floors do not represent nearly such a complicated field as carpeting. Wood comes in all its manifestations, hard and soft, in narrow or wide planks, parquet, mosaic and block, as well as the cheaper hardboard (masonite), particleboard and plywood. Then there are all the sheet and tile vinyls, composition and rubber tiles, corks and linoleums, as well as ceramic tiles, clay terracotta and quarry tiles, slate, brick, stone, terrazzo, travertine and marble. It is all a matter of price, suitability and aesthetics. Some of the vinyls and linoleums need no longer be thought of as substitutes for natural materials, but as beautiful floors in their own right – particularly some of the new Japanese vinyls.

LAYING NEW WOOD FLOORS

There is a large choice of both hard and soft woods for your new wooden floor. Hard woods include white and red oak (very popular), walnut, cherry, birch, poplar and maple (these last, whiter woods are in fact

LEFT: Herringbone-patterned coir matting provides an appropriate base for an exotically coloured and furnished room.

57

quite soft). Soft woods are pine (very cheap), larch, spruce, cedar, redwood and hemlock (the last two are quite hard). Some soft woods have a yellow-orange line (red oak has this too); toned down with a translucent stain or wash, this makes a beautiful background for stencils, borders or painted rugs.

Whatever wood you choose, it is most important that it should be properly dry and seasoned. You should also ensure that the moisture content is suitable for the kind of heating system you have in the room (for example, 10% to 14% moisture content in the wood with normal central heating; 6% to 8% if there is underfloor heating). I have little knowledge of how this can be tested, but if you make the proper enquiries, you at least sound as if you know what you are talking about and are less likely to be palmed off with inferior goods or service! All wood should be left unwrapped in the room in which it is to be used for at least two days before laying. Wide boards can be nailed to joists, and tongue-and-groove floorboards can be fitted together and 'secret' nailed either to joists or to a wooden sub-floor. Ready made or manufactured wood floors, such as strip or parquet, should be laid on level plywood or masonite sub-floors; wood block or mosaic floors can be laid straight on to concrete screed, plywood or particleboard.

Materials such as plywood, masonite, particleboard and chipboard, which are really meant for sub-floors, can, if properly sealed against water, be used as floors in their own right. They are cheap and can look quite handsome. Masonite (which you can buy in squares) can be painted and sealed; chip or particleboard and plywood can be stained, varnished and sealed. Both masonite and plywood squares can

be marbled or plain painted and then laid in checkerboard fashion.

Unless your new wooden floor is pre-sealed (as are most manufactured floors), all new and renovated wood must be finished with either two or three coats of polyurethane wood sealer or varnish, or several layers of wax polish.

LAYING MANUFACTURED FLOORING

Both plain vinyl and the slightly thicker linoleum flooring can be cut and inset to make some splendidly high profile floors. The sheet variety (which is available in various

A richly coloured Oriental rug under the chair by the piano softens the large expanse of parquet floor. Together with the flowers, the lamp shade, the plant stand and the painting, it adds warmth to a basically neutral room.

widths) can be laid very quickly on large spaces; tiles are better for smaller and more irregular areas. Although cutting and insetting are specialist skills, the results can look spectacular. The chief advantage of both vinyl and linoleum is that they are smooth and warm. They are also cheaper and easier to maintain than wood flooring. As they withstand damp, water and spills and can generally be cleaned with a quick, damp mop (avoid strong detergents), they are useful for entrance halls and corridors as well as kitchens, bathrooms and children's rooms. Apart from the plain colours (which allow you to make your own designs), vinyls come in a dazzling array of designs, some simulating natural materials such as wood, brick, marble, ceramic and quarry tiles. Cork tiles look warm and attractive, but need to be sealed for maximum practicality. Rubber tiles are good for rooms that need to be fairly soundproof, such as bathrooms and utility rooms, but are not good in kitchens. All of these floors can be laid on concrete or subfloors.

LAYING NATURAL FLOORS

Brick, ceramic, terracotta and quarry tile floors are particularly good for country or beach houses. They are especially good at withstanding water and mud, although they are hard to stand on for any sustained period of time in a kitchen. Slate and marble look particularly handsome in entrance halls or bathrooms, and they are ideal for all floors in the sun.

Brick and stone should not be sealed and are best just kept swept and washed. All natural floors should be laid on concrete screed. Do not attempt to lay ceramic wall tiles on to floors: they crack easily and are too slippery. Ceramic floor tiles are thicker, egg glazed and often textured for enhanced safety.

Rugs

✔ Instant room-enliveners, rugs add warmth and softness to hard floors. Always secure them with Velcro strips or non-slip backing underneath or they can cause lethal accidents. Old and rare Orientals and antique needlework rugs, as well as modern rugs designed by famous painters and rug makers, should never be put on floors which get much use. These works of art are splendid investments, but can easily deteriorate with wear and tear.

The various weaves are as follows:

✔ TRADITIONAL PILE RUGS Made by knotting tufts of wool and, more rarely, silk, these come mainly from the Middle and Far East – the more knots per square inch or centimetre, the more costly the rug. Various characteristics distinguish rugs from different regions. Persian or Iranian rugs have stylized geometric or floral designs (each village or town with its own motifs and shades), typically in deep reds and blues. Turkish carpets have a similarly rich colouring, often with a particular green. Many small Turkish prayer rugs have an arch design supported by pillars. Chinese rugs are generally much thicker, often sculpted, and have Oriental motifs of dragons, flowers, lotus trees and butterflies. French Savonnerie rugs have cut pile in the Oriental style. Greek 'flokatis' and Finish 'ryas' are both shaggy pile rugs. In the West, many hand- and machine-made pile rugs are produced.

✔ BRAIDED, HOOKED AND RAG RUGS These hand-made rugs are made from old scraps of wool and used fabrics. Braided rugs are either oval or round. Hooked rugs are made from looped pile worked in a deliberately naive design. Rag rugs are usually made in irregular stripes of varying colours. Old American rugs in all these types are highly prized. Luxurious modern examples are made in Portugal.

✔ NEEDLEWORK RUGS Eighteenth- and nineteenth-century French (such as Aubusson) and English needlework rugs are collectors' pieces. Excellent modern versions are made in Portugal and Romania, often to order.

✔ FLAT WEAVES Woven without a pile, these rugs are made of cotton or wool, a mixture of the two or, very occasionally, silk. They are also usually considerably cheaper than pile rugs, although antique flat weave rugs such as kelims from Persia, Turkey and Afghanistan are much prized. Modern kelims are still produced in the Middle East from work in geometric designs and warm, rich vegetable-derived colours that mellow well.

✔ DHURRIES Another type of traditional flat-weave rug, generally made in India from cotton. They can often be reversed successfully and come in a vast range of colours and styles. Mexican flat-weave 'serapes' are coarser, often fringed, and normally very colourful.

WINDOWS

Great advances have been made recently with windows. However graceful and elegant old windows may look, they can be 'energy sieves', letting in winter drafts and leaking out precious warmed air. They can also let in too much heat and sun in summer. New windows have infinitely superior glazing techniques, notably with the now almost standard low emissivity, or low-E variety. This means double-glazed panes with a microscopically thin metallic film between the two layers of glass which reflects radiant heat. In winter, low-E glass allows light and heat entering the room to become absorbed in the walls, floors and furnishings with no reciprocal heat loss. At night the stored energy is re-radiated into the room at lower temperatures but cannot escape, as before, through the glass. In the summer, low-E glass helps to keep interiors cool and prevents furniture near the windows from fading. Houses can therefore now be designed with an enormous amount of glass without fear of energy loss, as in previous generations; and energy-efficient windows, available in both old and new styles, can now replace old, inefficient models.

Some windows need little or nothing in the way of decorative treatment: those that are not over-looked, those with a beautiful view, elegant arched windows on stairs and landings, narrow slits of glass, small ovals or rounds and stained and etched glass windows that are often unopenable anyway. In these cases, a decorative object on a sill – a single flower in a vase, an old jug, a coloured or engraved decanter, a small lamp, or some sculptural object – is better than attempting any fabric or alternative treatment.

Most of us, however, have to cope with rather ordinary, and

ABOVE: Gathered and fringed Austrian blinds or shades.are highly practical as they can show off the good lines of a window as well as disguising any faults of proportion. These blinds have been in vogue since the eighteenth century.
BELOW: Glass or wood shelves across a window give privacy with and offer excellent display space.

ABOVE: Long curtains, puddling slightly on to the floor, are suspended from brass curtain rings looped over a Neo classical brass pole. This is a simple and elegant treatment for long, graceful windows
BELOW: a swagged and tailed valance over tied-back curtains meeting in the middle of the window gives a much more formal and elaborate look.

Natural-coloured Roman blinds are fixed directly on to the frames of the pairs of French windows. This arrangement allows doors to be opened without obstruction from window treatments.

sometimes rather awkward, windows that are overlooked. For cheap and effective solutions here are some suggestions.

DIFFERENT WINDOWS, DIFFERENT TREATMENTS

Well proportioned windows that have a pretty view and let in a lot of welcome light can be destroyed by heavy or over-elaborate treatments – something that the Victorians did all too often. In the eighteenth century, graceful windows were mostly dressed with pull-up curtains or Austrian blinds or shades, which provided protection and privacy without losing proportion. Good-looking windows are still well served by fabric shades or blinds of some sort, from Austrian to Roman or roller shades. They can, of course, be made to look more dressy with swags or pelmets attached to the top of the window. If you want to make the windows look longer, without losing too much daylight, it is a good idea to hang toppings of this sort form the ceiling or the cornice, if there is one. Again, if you want to make square windows look longer and more graceful, but do not want to afford full-length curtains, you can keep the shades of whatever sort, and hang 'dress' curtains at the sides of the windows, which can be permanently looped back with tie backs.

Another useful trick with a pair of squarish windows, especially in a long narrow room where seating arrangements can be limited and awkward, is to build a frame around the windows, deep enough to add a window seat. Not only does this make the window seem more graceful and provide extra seating, but it can also give you some subtle storage if you have the window seats made with lift-up lids; the newly created alcoves either side of the windows can also

61

A collection of old soda-water siphons and cut-glass decanters arranged on a window-sill and shelf remove the need for a conventional fabric treatment.

be made into storage space for drinks, records, discs, tapes, toys or whatever else.

Windows, or French doors and windows that open inwards (or tilt), are clearly always going to be difficult to open when blinds are down or curtains drawn. The only possible thing to do is to make sure that curtain headings or blind fixings are extra long and are mounted well above the window (and if that is possible – sometimes such windows are tucked in just under the ceiling anyway, in which case you either have to mount a shade of some description right on to the frame, or, if there is any sort of window recess or alcove, just in front). If you *can* mount fixings well above the window, and keep long curtains well looped back to the sides of the windows, it will at least mean that you can open the window during the day without getting it tangled up in the treatment.

Different sized windows next door to each other are best treated in the same way, with curtains or long vertical blinds. Run the pole, rod, heading, valance or pelmet right across both windows, with long curtains looped back on either side, or one very big curtain looped

back to the side of the large window or the vertical blinds pulled to one side. As an alternative, treat each window as an abstract shape and give it a neat shade such as a roller or Roman fabric blind, a mini or slatted blind, or even crisp pairs of white painted shutters.

Bay windows often have deep window sills or radiators underneath, which long curtains will obstruct, thereby losing heat. With these, use Roman, roller or Austrian blinds on the windows themselves and have a pair of dress curtains looped back on either side, if you still want the effect of long curtains.

Arched windows that need to be covered always look best with a treatment that mirrors their shape. Curved tracks with curtains are ideal here, but the curtains must always be kept looped back. Try to use a contrast lining, and loop the fabric back either at the bottom of the curve or half way down the window. You could also use an Austrian blind in a light, filmy fabric, with an arched track.

Windows with an unattractive outlook can be screened with a transparent or slatted shade that still lets in light with draped-back curtains at the side, voile or muslin under-curtains, café curtains (short curtains suspended from a rod fixed half way down the window), or with shutters, kept half open.

DRESSING UP FABRIC WINDOW TREATMENTS

Existing window treatments can be dressed up in various ways. You can add a length of fringe down each of the leading edges of curtains, an inset border, or a double border in a contrast colour grosgrain ribbon or binding. Tie-backs in any style are an embellishment, as are contrast linings to curtains, which show when you loop the fabric back. If curtains or blinds do

Swags hung straight from the ceiling, and bordered Roman blinds in thin sheeting material make short windows look long.

not have a pelmet or valance, you can add a draped swag over a pole or a wooden pelmet covered with matching wallpaper or fabric or painted another colour. A pair of over- or under-curtains in contrasting fabrics, or a contrasting plain shade or blind edged with a curtain fabric, can make a decided difference. Windows, and the way you treat them, are vital to a room, so it is worth varying the pace, as it were, from time to time.

SOME ALTERNATIVES

Curtains, blinds and shutters are not the only treatments for windows. You can hang a collection of plants in baskets from a brass or wooden rod suspended on long brackets across the top of the window frame. A leafy plant could be placed on a fairly narrow, but deeply recessed window. You can fix a number of glass shelves across a window for coloured or plain glass objects, perhaps intermingled with plants. A window with a spectacular view that is not overlooked can be treated like a picture frame and painted a different colour from the walls. Alternatively, it could be given mirrored reveals to reflect even more facets of the view.

SOFT FURNISHINGS

Comfort is probably the key word in decorating today and much of it is, or can be, provided by seating and bedding.

Because of the exigencies of the human frame, however, one person's comfort is another person's discomfort; truly comfortable furniture is very much a question of feel rather than taste. Although people might be tempted to choose sofas and upholstered chairs for their looks, their proportions might be all wrong for them, or right for one member of a family with, say, short legs and quite wrong for another with long legs. Interestingly, the only chairs of mine which got whole-hearted approbation were some upholstered dining chairs made specially tall for my handsome round pedestal dining table which is higher than normal. Guests invariably remarked on the comfort of my chairs, and I concluded that, since the chairs were deep in the seat as well as tall (most people had the sensation of their legs dangling) they were reminded of the comforting days of their childhood.

The only other comfortable chair by almost universal acclaim is the wide seated *bergère*, produced in the time of Louis XV; though hardly a chair you sink into, it seems to be ergonomically correct.

CHOOSING UPHOLSTERY

Choosing sofas and armchairs from scratch, as it were, gives you the chance to think about the habits of your family and friends. Some people like to lie out at full stretch on long sofas with plenty of soft pillows or cushions and low, wide

RIGHT: Different patterns but similar colours in the throws and shawls make this old chair look comfortably inviting and suit the general feel of the room.

arms that make good head rests. Others like to curl up on a sofa with deep seats and low backs. Others still prefer to sit upright with their back and neck supported. Short people need low, shallowish chairs; tall people, deep, higher seated chairs. Older people need firmish chairs with sturdy arms so they can rise more easily. Given all these quite common needs, you will see that your home will need all sorts of seating including sofas, comfortable club chairs, a wing chair, some firm *bergère*-type chairs, and perhaps a rocking chair.

It is very important when you are buying upholstery to spend a long time testing it out from all angles. Do not feel embarrassed, or that you are keeping assistants waiting unnecessarily. Good upholstery is expensive enough to be considered an investment in both money and future comfort, so you have to make good long-term choices.

TABLES AND TABLECLOTHS

The skirted table must be one of the most useful adjuncts to any room, except perhaps the nursery where the cloth is likely to be unceremoniously yanked off. The cloth – or cloth and over-cloth (most such tables look more interesting with the double whammy, so to speak) –

will add colour, pattern and/or texture to the space, acting as a balance to the other colour schemes in the room. The table will hold a lamp and objects, as well as being a convenient nearby surface for a chair, sofa, or bed. The table itself need only be utilitarian chipboard, but the cloth can be used to hide the television, VCR, tapes and children's toys, which, when visitors arrive, can be swept swiftly under the table!

Since dining tables are apt to be expensive, you can make do with a cheap, preferably round, table covered with a permanent long cloth of heavy material, topped by an easily

Left: A voile canopy draped over a brass boss fixed high on the wall softens the somewhat severe lines of the sleigh-bed, as does the skirted table by its side.

laundered over-cloth. A daytime roundtable in a library or study can be turned into a dining room with the addition of a long tablecloth.

Tablecloths range from the colourful to the exotic. A scarf top fits well as an over-cloth for a round table, and it can be dressed up with a bordering fringe, tassel or bobbles sewn on to the pointed ends. The bottom cloth can also be fringed or bordered. Oblong tables look best with more crisply tailored cloths, and a contrasting over-cloth.

BED TREATMENTS

Beds should be chosen for their comfort and quality – the more expensive a mattress and box spring, the longer and better it should serve you. How you dress a bed can make all the difference to a bedroom's character. Fortunately, given the eclecticism of linen suppliers and the myriad designs now available, making a beautiful bed is not a difficult task.

Manufacturers have for years observed people decorating with sheets because they were the cheapest way of buying a large amount of fabric; now they provide practically everything for the bedroom except the carpet and the bed. Sheets, bedspreads, duvet covers, bed frills and pillows come in delicate *broderies Anglaises*, lace and embroidered white linens from China that would make any bed look inviting. Florals, dark solids, stripes and plaids and animal skin prints also abound, as do various collections of fabrics and sheets with co-ordinating fabrics for window blinds, valances, bed frills, canopies, bedside tablecloths, pillows, and cushions as well as wallpapers and borders.

Four-Poster Beds

✔ Four-poster beds, magnificently carved and decorated, were prized household possessions from late medieval times up to the nineteenth century. It is now quite possible to give beds elaborate-looking treatment with clever, and not necessarily expensive, use of fabrics. A fabric four-poster can be made by nailing a narrow wooden frame to the ceiling (as long as it is not too high) immediately above the bed, making it just slightly larger than the made-up mattress. You can then fit a valance to it with velcro or tacks. This can be simply a bought bed skirt or ruffle stretched on to the frame..

✔ Of course, if you actually *possess* a four-poster and want to make a canopy for it, you could use some light-diffusing fabric like voile, muslin or *broderie Anglaise*, with an attached frill some 30 cm (12 in) deep. Unless you want a crisp, flat valance or pelmet, you will need to allow at least one and a half times the total length and width of the bed for the fullness required for a frill.

✔ Once the canopy or valance is made, attach four hemmed lengths of fabric to each corner, again with velcro, letting them either break slightly on the ground or hang straight with gentle tie-backs of some sort. For the bed curtains, you could use patterned 'King Size' sheets, filmy voile, lace, tight-woven muslin or some altogether more elaborate fabric with contrast lining and borders and other trimmings.

✔ Another good effect for either single or double beds is to drape a canopy over a pole attached from the ceiling at right angles over the head of the bed. Using a double width of fabric, with a length corresponding to the distance from the floor of one side of the bed, drape the material over the pole and down to the floor the opposite side. This fabric can be trimmed and lined or just unlined and used with tie backs or looped over brass bosses or wooden dowels. A single bed can be positioned, French style, long ways against a wall and the fabric draped from a pole so that it falls at either end of the bed. You can achieve much the same effect by using a crown or *couronne* instead of a pole. You can buy shaped pieces of track especially for this or just gather a tiny pelmet on to a short rod. Finally you can make a half-tester (which means the canopy reaches only to the turn-down of the bed), with side curtains at each corner.

✔ Velcro is extremely useful for simulating four-poster beds provided you do not have too high a ceiling. Fix a slim wooden frame to the ceiling slightly overlapping the bed beneath. Attach a valance (or even a ready-made bed frill) to it, and then attach four curtains to touch the ground at all four corners. If you do have a proper four-poster you could use a light-diffusing fabric over the top, or a pukka sunray-pleated canopy with an attached frill or straight valance at the sides. Alternatively just attach a frill or straight-sided pelmet to the actual frame.

DECORATING
recipes

Whatever the size and type of your home, it will inevitably consist of a series of rooms that serve distinct functions. The decoration of each room must obviously be suitable for the use to which it is put, but ideally should make some concessions to the overall look. This can be difficult to acheive if people with different tastes share the same house; nevertheless, it is worth considering, when you start one room, how it will work with others completed later. First and foremost, however, should come practical considerations: a hall needs somewhere to hang coats and stand umbrellas; a living room must be furnished in such a way as to withstand regular wear and tear; workrooms need adequate task lighting; kitchens should be as ergonomic as possible, and children's rooms adaptable enough to accommodate them throughout their growing years.

LEFT: This large and sumptuous hall is provided with every luxury: a sofa, tables, umbrella stands, a mirror and elegant plants.

RIGHT: Anomalous furniture is ideally situated in halls where it can often serve a practical purpose; blue and yellow paint in this child's room is nicely linked by the duck border just above the dado; the vertiginous feeling of this cellar room is echoed by the strong diagonals of the tiles on the stair risers.

HALLS AND STAIRCASES

Understandably, most people would rather spend their money on the decoration and furnishing of rooms other than entrances and exits. Nevertheless, since halls or foyers are the first introduction to a home as well as the last space you pass through when you leave, you should certainly try to make them as warm, welcoming and good looking as possible. And as stairways almost always lead off an entrance hall, they are generally best treated together as a whole.

Fortunately, at least as far as the average decorating budget is concerned, entrance halls tend to be fairly small, especially in cities. Occasionally you can get large, light and airy spaces, sometimes with the additional bonus of a fireplace, but more often than not these areas tend to be somewhat dull with little room for furniture other than a small table and chair. If you are fortunate, you may be able to fit in some sort of cupboard, or at least a coat rack.

A splendid wooden figure stands at the foot of the staircase below an Egyptian painting and a motley collection of hats. Note the wash of light across the treads, so important for safety.

Given these limitations, the most suitable points to concentrate on, both for halls and staircases, are probably the lighting, walls, ceilings, woodwork and flooring.

LIGHTING

As with any other wiring (such as for telephone lines or burglar alarms), lighting arrangements must be in place before the decoration is started. In any later changes, wall and ceiling treatments could be ruined. In halls and passages, and particularly on staircases, lighting is as important for safety's sake as for welcoming first impressions. It is wise also to

ensure that the *outside* of the front door is equally well lit.

Recessed downlights or, if you are going to hang pictures or objects on your walls, a mixture of recessed downlights and wall-washers, are the ideal because they take up little visual space, do not collect flies and dust (as pendant and bowl-shaped fixtures do) and will go with any style of furnishings. But they are best attached to a dimmer switch (which also means that they can be dimmed but still left on at night for the comfort and safety of the old and young). For particularly valued paintings or sculpture, if you have the funds available, there is nothing better than the beautiful and focussed lighting provided by framing projectors.

Recessed lights may, however, be inappropriate for various reasons: a ceiling recess which is too shallow; a concrete ceiling which cannot be pierced; not enough spare money for their purchase and installation; or a rental agreement which does not allow you to play around with the home very much. In these cases, there are certainly reasonable alternatives.

Track lighting, in which the spots are angled at will, is one solution. The track should be trim and the spots small and neat. Track lighting has the huge advantage that it can be surface-mounted on to a single ceiling (or wall) outlet, yet provide maximum flexibility. If, due to financial or aesthetic constraints, you have to make do with a single central ceiling outlet, at least be sure to use a powerful bulb with a dimmer switch and as interesting a fitting as possible. You might also be able to supplement the lighting with a table lamp and, possibly, uplights situated in corners.

This elegant staircase is well provided with light by day, as well as by night. Note how the risers on the stone stairs are painted white to make them stand out, just as the risers on the terracotta-tiled stairs opposite are painted a much paler colour for reasons of safety.

If you just want to light the space – and not any pictures or other objects on the walls – wall fixtures that throw light down as well as up are good in hallways and corridors, and especially on staircases where it is essential to light up each tread. But here again the wires have to be chased into the walls and the exact height and spacing of fixtures decided upon before decoration. The only wall lights that can be fixed satisfactorily after decoration are swing-arm brass lamps with slim brass tubes to conceal the wires or flex.

If your hallway is in darkness or deep gloom most of the time, as in so many apartment buildings and terrace houses, try to use as much concealed light as possible. Uplights can be placed in corners and behind furniture, and lights set above deep cornices or, if there are no existing cornices, behind some sort of purpose-built pelmet or valance. This treatment is especially useful for walls lined with bookshelves, as it lights the books as well as the space. Additional swing-arm lamps can also be mounted for extra light on the uprights of bookshelves.

You can also extend borrowed daylight (and the general sense of space) by substituting French doors for the solid variety or by cutting out archway 'windows' on either side of an archway, or long slits from floor to ceiling in non-load bearing walls.

A telephone on a table, desk or shelf in the hall obviously needs a lamp nearby, or at least a light

The intricately painted curved chest makes a splendid focal point in this foyer, as well as being usefully capacious. The apricot of the walls repeats the colour of the roses on the chest's panels.

trained on it, for easy reading of numbers in telephone books as well as for writing messages.

DECORATION

To make a hallway or foyer as welcoming and striking as possible, you should choose warm colourings and interesting treatments. In moderate and cold climates, terracottas, deep roses, bright yellows, reds, apricots and tawny colours look good and, with the liberal use of wood, natural textures and Oriental or other handsome rugs for floors, are suitable in both the town and country. Another possibility for hall and landing floors is a painted *trompe l'oeil* rug, perhaps with an Oriental design or one picking up the wallpaper or fabric. Fun and cheerful, this solution is also very practical since it is easy to clean and will obviously never slip or ruck up,

the safety hazard of most rugs.

All surfaces should be as tough and as resistant to wear and tear as possible. After all, people will be coming in from outside, and objects and furniture will need to be moved in and out on occasion. Painted walls should be covered in washable paint, and wallpapers should be washable vinyl or, alternatively, should be given a coat of toughening polyurethane.

In a hot climate you will almost certainly need the coolness and freshness of whites, blues, greens, pale yellows, buffs and creams. Whatever the climate, however, don't forget that architectural details such as cornices, dados or chair rails always add interest to the walls.

A large mirror, or a mirrored area, is useful in a hallway, not just for examining appearances at entrances and exits, but for the light and space it reflects. Halls, staircases and landing walls will also absorb any amount of treasures – paintings, prints, photographs, framed objects, collections of this and that – quite apart from wall-hung rugs and textiles. If the space is large enough, a ceiling-high breakfront bookcase can provide useful storage cupboards below, and floor-to-waist-height bookshelves are as practical as they are decorative.

FURNISHINGS

Your furnishing needs will, of course, depend on the space available, your pocket book and your chosen style. A table or chest, a chair and, if possible, some kind of cupboard, or at least a coat rack or a row of hooks, are obviously desirable. As first impressions are what count, you can afford to choose pieces of furniture as much for their idiosyncratic looks as for their practicality.

LIVING ROOMS

Not unnaturally, we all want our living rooms to look good, feel comfortable and reflect our sense of style. But how do you accomplish this if your family comprises different generations with conflicting tastes and needs: children who care little about decoration, animals who care even less and parents with different interests, pursuits and preoccupations?

FAMILIES VERSUS ELEGANCE

You may be fortunate enough to have a den, library, family or guest room which can act as a casual, feet-up, leave-the-toys-out sort of room. If so, you can afford to design, and more importantly to maintain, a more elegant living room. In this case, however, the old-fashioned 'withdrawing' or 'drawing room' might be the more appropriate term: 'living room' suggests something of the hurly-burly of a room for living. But if you have only one general room, which might have to accommodate a dining table as well, you will have to think long and hard about how to plan its use. Ask yourself a lot of salient questions and be realistic about the answers. For example, if you have children who cannot be kept out of the living room entirely, then your dream of having a colour scheme of plain pastels, whites or creams is clearly impractical.

But take heart. You could still achieve a fresh, pale and pretty room by using close-patterned fabrics that will show less dirt

RIGHT: The pristine white upholstery in this blue and white room is maintained by covering all the seating with the simplest form of slip-covers – large white dust sheets.

ABOVE: Skirted tables are invaluable in every living room where there is enough space. They add colour, pattern and sometimes exoticism, as with the fringed shawl here, and provide space for an extra table lamp as well as for displaying objects. The actual table can be very cheap, so that you have all the usefulness of a handsome piece of furniture at a fraction of the cost.

ABOVE RIGHT: Valuable storage is provided in this room both by the built-in wooden shelves and the free-standing bookshelves beside them. These are used for objects and plants, as well as books, and are decoratve in their own right against the plain white walls. The curved-sided black serving trolley is an extremely useful item in any room with a dining table.

afford them, balance the height in a room and, like drop-front desks, secretaries and chests of drawers, can provide a good deal of extra storage. You can always add skirted tables with long cloths to conceal general family bric-à-brac.

SPACE-SAVING STORAGE

If the room is very small, glass shelves may be the answer. They can provide storage for books and, with a deeper waist-height shelf, a place for TV, stereo, VCR and drinks, without taking up much visual space. At night uplights can light the shelves from beneath and provide sparkle.

Mirrored alcoves either side of a chimney breast can be a space-stretcher in a small room. They will double the apparent length of the walls and, if the chimney faces or is adjacent to a window, will also reflect natural window light.

Another space-saving trick is to build in window seats with lift-up lids, thereby effectively providing both extra storage and seating with little apparent loss of floor space. An easy way to do this is to construct a deep frame around the windows from floor to ceiling (which can make them look tall and graceful even though they may be square), add upholstered seats at an appropriate height and fill in the space beneath with hinged doors (wallpapered in with the rest of the walls to appear nearly invisible). You could thus create a number of concealed shelves, while at the same time adding to the potential seating in your room.

LIGHTING

The exact position of electrical points and outlets should ideally have been worked out on your original floor plan (see p. 24). This is the only way to avoid the

than solid colours. You might also have two sets of slip-covers made for each piece of upholstery: one set on and one replacement for when the first has to go to the cleaners. Some upholstery manufacturers sell sofas and chairs with spare slip-covers, which saves you having to have them specially tailored for the piece. Instead of impractical light-coloured carpets, you could have bleached or pale-painted wooden floors with easily-cleaned rugs. Vinyl or linoleum in light colours can be washed and can look very fine when skilfully cut with designs and borders.

STORAGE

If you have children, or any sort of extended family, you will need to introduce as much storage as you possibly can, especially if you have to eat in the room as well. Modern wall-storage systems can house bookshelves, cupboards for drinks, glasses, china and cutlery, space for electronic equipment such as stereos, TV and VCR, a desk unit and so on. But if you prefer a more traditional room you can build in bookshelves with a deep breakfront for storage. Handsome old *armoires* and bureau-bookcases, if you can

untidiness and hazard of trailing wires or flexes across the floor.

The same careful pre-planning applies to any recessed ceiling lighting. If you have particular works of art you wish to highlight in this way, you will need to work out exactly where you are going to hang or place them so that the relevant light, or lights, can be positioned accordingly. An alternative, however, is to position tiny portable spot lights on mantlepieces, tables and the floor. You can also install floor lamps equipped with two or three adjustable spots; vertical lengths of track on walls are effective too, as are horizontal tracks on ceilings or along skirting or base boards.

ARRANGEMENT

How you arrange your furniture and possessions can make a profound difference to the look of a space and its general sense of balance. It is always best to experiment first with pieces of furniture drawn to scale on your floor plan (see p. 24). The important thing is for the room to work comfortably – both visually and physically.

Any arrangement will depend on how you are to use that room. If you entertain regularly, you will have to ensure that you have sufficient seating for everybody to sit down. This may mean providing extra seating when required, with furniture groupings that can expand and contract accordingly.

It helps to work outward from the focal point of a room. A working fireplace is the ideal focal point. The reading/conversation

(see p. 24).

LEFT: The symmetrically hung collection of botanical prints is offset by the softer arrangement of pillows or cushions on the bench below. The miscellany of colours and designs makes a pleasant sitting area in this room.

area will then depend on the size of the room and the position of the fireplace. One scenario is to have a large comfortable sofa placed opposite the fire with, say, a love seat to one side of the hearth and two armchairs on the other. Another would be to have two love seats facing each other and two armchairs facing the mantlepiece. If the room is very spacious, one large sofa could face the mantlepiece with two love seats on either side and assorted armchairs, club, wing and occasional chairs in the spaces in between. If there is no fireplace you might try making the focal point around a window with a view. If the television seems to be the focus, then try to place the set in an attractive storage unit or cabinet, so that the seating groups still look elegant.

BOOKS DO FURNISH A ROOM

In the eighteenth and nineteenth century, libraries started out as rooms for the housing and enjoyment of books; but because almost all members of the household preferred to be in them, libraries took on the guise of family rooms. Anyone who seriously wanted to read and write in peace invariably had to create a new room for the purpose, such as a study or workroom. Some of the best and most inviting living rooms today are often a cross between a library and a sitting room, full of books and clutter.

It is wise to think about the shape of your room before building bookshelves. A thin room with shelves across its longer wall can feel like a tunnel, and remedying a mistake of this sort can prove extremely expensive. Also be wary of building more bookshelves than you could ever hope to fill – rows of gappy shelves can look a little forlorn!

Details and Accessories

✔ A well-dressed room gives as much pleasure as a well-dressed person. But however good the colour scheme, however grand and luxurious the furniture, and however harmonious and flexible the arrangements, it is the details and accessories that finally make the room personal, memorable and a pleasure to be in. And the most deeply restful rooms are those in which all the furnishings and objects weld gently together, with no one thing jumping out at you, no sense of conspicuous expenditure.

✔ In the best looking rooms, even with a pleasing lived-in clutter, what counts is the harmony of the details. Tablecloths and curtains should be just the right length; the lighting should be gentle but provide interesting contrasts; plants and flowers should be fresh and not overarranged; and trimmings and borders should nicely offset the fabrics. In an ideal room real flames should flicker in the fireplace, the log baskets should be stacked with firewood and the whole place should smell of woodsmoke and scented blooms.

✔ The objects and works of art you choose to surround youself with should be things you really care for and that feel right for the style of the room – not items that you think will impress your friends and acquaintances, or which seem to be fashionable at the moment. Unless objects have some personal, nostalgic or sentimental connection for you and your family, they can make your living room, however beautifully furnished, feel more like a hotel than a home.

LIVING ROOM MAKEOVER – STAGE 1

To show how spaces can be adapted over the years to fulfil varying roles, as well as to demonstrate different theories and styles, I have chosen a living room which has undergone a number of changes. We can imagine that it was part of a house inherited by a young couple from an elderly aunt. Like a lot of houses built in the 1920s and before, the house had been stripped of most of its architectural details during the 1950s. With only a very limited budget to begin with the decision was taken to make the living room look as good as possible. So the first step was to put back the details – adding inexpensive polystyrene mouldings, a better mantlepiece and proper French doors. Once the floor had been stripped, the wiring attended to and the walls papered, only minimal funds were left for the furnishings.

ABOVE: A small desk area is provided by the simple expedient of fixing a triangular piece of wood into the corner and painting it blue and white. A junk-shop chair is painted white, as are the lengths of polystyrene mouldings used as a chair rail.

ABOVE: In this budget-conscious room, an old sofa is given a blue and white cotton slip-cover and the same material covers a round table and some pillows, softening the cane chairs. An old painted trunk acts as a coffee table, and a white rocking chair is given blue stripes.

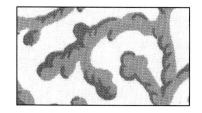

Blue and white cotton in an allover pattern is used as a slip-cover for the sofa as well as for the cloth on the table by the wing chair.

Blue denim is used for the cushions on the cane chairs and sofa. Bright and practical, it complements the other blue hues in the room.

Highly polished floors, even those simulated in vinyl, invariably have an attractive, warm tone and blend in easily with almost any decorative treatment.

TOP: A graceful mantlepiece lends tone and distinction to any living room. The table/extra desk is just a plate-glass top on simple trestles.

BOTTOM: Lit from below, plate-glass shelves on brackets give sparkle.

LIVING ROOM MAKEOVER – STAGE 2

Here is the same living room some years later. We can imagine that the couple have saved enough money to be able to make various improvements to the furnishings. The blue walls and the needlework rug in front of the fireplace remain, as do the glass bookshelves and the glass table. The wicker furniture, however, is now in to the porch, the triangular corner desk and chair have gone, and the painted chest that was used as a coffee table has been put in another room. In their place are two comfortable club chairs and a wing chair slip-covered with a clear blue and white cotton with a relatively large scale pattern which has also been used for the new, grander window treatments. A butler's tray has been found for use as a coffee table; an interesting nineteenth-century French writing table and chair, a pretty side table and some nice old prints have been bought for the walls. The room now looks far more elegant.

ABOVE: The new curtains sport a fairly elaborate swag and tails, and are tied back to take full advantage of the outside view. Notice the juxtaposition of the larger blue and white print with the smaller scale print used as a slip-cover for the sofa.

ABOVE: Comfortable club chairs are slip-covered in clear blue denim. The new wing chair, matching the curtains, helps to make the room look more formal and better cared-for.

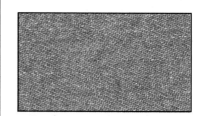

Blue denim that appeared on the cushions only (in stage 1) makes a far greater impact when used as slip-covers for the matching club chairs.

The blue and white striped satin fabric on the chair at the writing table has an elegant Regency feel in keeping with the style of the new formal window treatment.

A large-scale blue and white cotton with an attractive floral print is used for the slip cover on the wing chair as well as for the new curtains.

TOP: The triangular piece of painted wood that formerly did duty as a desk has been replaced with a nineteenth-century Louis Philippe French writing table and a matching chair.
BOTTOM: Various objects and prints have been distributed around the room.

LIVING ROOM MAKEOVER – STAGE 3

The couple's ultimate preference is for traditional, Victorian-style furnishings (antiques from the nineteenth century being more generally available and better priced than those of earlier periods). The glass bookshelves and table have been removed and the wall-colour changed to a rose with a marbled green paper beneath the chair rail. The mouldings remain white, but the fireplace and skirting (or base) boards have also been marbled. A fine Victorian painting has pride-of-place over the mantlepiece, a club fender has been added to the fireplace and girandoles to the walls. A pair of palms are planted in brass buckets, and a variety of interesting period prints put up in place of the smaller classical ones (of stage 2). The lighting is gentle, primarily from the table lamps situated discretely in the corners of the room.

82

ABOVE: The room, formerly with a blue wallpaper, has now been painted a deep rose. The blue and white fabrics have been replaced by a richer green, blue and rose combination. Marbling has been applied, and the overall effect is of a high-Victorian living room.

ABOVE: The Louis-Philippe writing table is now behind a nineteenth-century sofa, and a Louis Quinze-style *secrétaire* has been placed between the windows. The side-table and occasional chair have heavily carved frames, and the rug has been changed for an AUBUSSON.

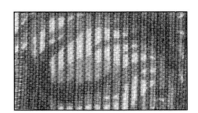

A richly patterned blue, green and rose floral-design fabric replaces the blue and white swagged curtains.

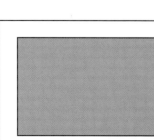

Green marble 'faux finish' paper is used to form a dado in obvious contrast with the texture and colour of the walls above.

This rich, warm paint colour is of a distinctively Victorian salmon-pink hue and provides an excellent counterpoint to the more restful greens.

TOP: The mantlepiece is now marbled, and pilasters flank the chimney-breast. The glass bookshelves have given way to an attractive brass lectern

BOTTOM: Other additions are the wall brackets, the club fender and the palms.

ROOMS FOR WORK AND PLAY

Rooms that have a set function are some of the nicest to furnish and decorate. They might be a study for writing and reading, a den for watching TV or playing cards, a music room for playing an instrument or listening to music, a studio for painting, sculpting or carving, a nursery for toys or an office for work. In each case, there is a purpose or function that has to be catered for.

Usually such rooms are small and, unlike small living rooms which people tend to strive to make look more spacious, the scale is an asset rather than a disadvantage. In small rooms with a set function, the lack of square footage makes for intimacy and a degree of cosiness, provided, of course, that there is a sufficient amount of storage space.

Interestingly, the more furniture you pack into small rooms the more welcoming they seem. In a study, for instance, you can line walls with shelves for books, TV, VCR and stereo, have a comfortable sofa (or sofabed for overflow guests), a writing table or desk and comfortable desk chair, an armchair, club or wing chair, a stool or ottoman and maybe one or two small occasional or slipper chairs. If you have a fireplace, surround it with a club fender for extra seating with no real loss of floor space.

These rooms benefit from warm, rich colours and a stimulating mixture of different patterns and textures: paisleys and checks, stripes and plaids, corduroys and velvets.

RIGHT: A cool and efficient room in which to work with its predominantly white space, serious writing table and well-stocked ceiling-high shelves.

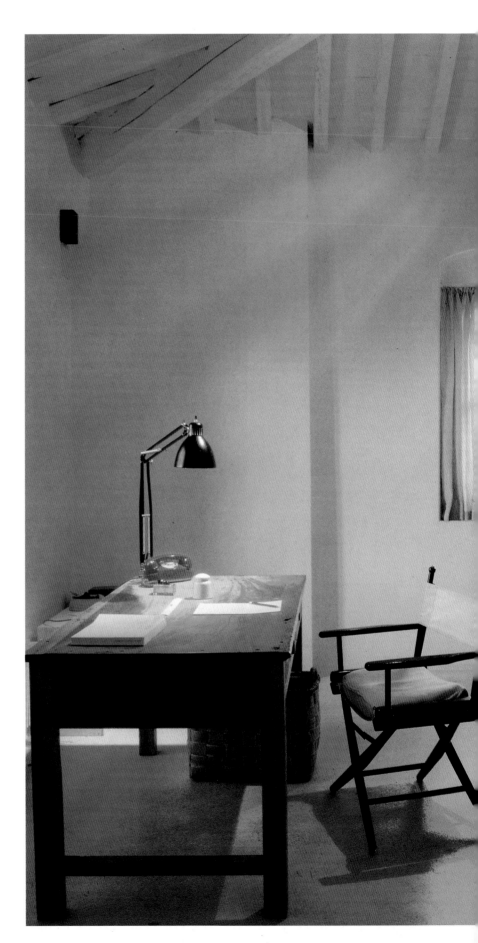

Home Offices

✔ Since it is now so easy to work from home while remaining in constant touch with the office, more and more people are choosing to do just this. But unless a home is large enough to set aside a separate room, you will need somehow to insert efficient working space into part of your living room, bedroom or dining room. At the same time you will have to be ingenious about disguising equipment that is not in use.

✔ A home office can be successfully incorporated into a bedroom, with little visible sign. You can use a pull-out work surface (for a computer and printer) hidden in a shelving system within a cupboard. A drop leaf desk can be substituted for a chest (to hide all signs of work paraphernalia), and window seats with lift-up lids can be fitted with filing cabinets underneath. There are also some handsome modern stationery units on the market, which, though by no means cheap,

make it possible for you to turn almost any room into efficient work space.

✔ If you are going to convert space for working from home you will need to plan it very carefully. An attic, basement, garage or summer house, for example, might well need wall insulation, new windows, a good ventilation system, rewiring to accommodate electrical machinery, new flooring (anti-static for computers), proper heating or cooling systems, and, of course, maximum storage space. It is almost certainly a good idea in a family home to install a second telephone line, especially if you have a fax machine or modem.

✔ Home offices might sound alarmingly expensive, but you could be pleasantly surprised to find that what you save on commuting expenses and time over a couple of years amortizes the expenditure very well.

DUAL-PURPOSE ROOMS

Whatever their prime function, most of these work-cum-play rooms can have a number of uses.

STUDY-GUEST ROOMS

By using a sofabed or daybed, rather than a normal sofa, you can easily make a study, den or workroom double as an occasional guest room. You could always provide a couple of brass hooks on the back of the door for clothes hanging. If there is room, you could add a chest of drawers; failing that, you could perhaps leave a drawer empty in a drop-leaf desk or even just clear a cupboard shelf.

Make sure there is a good light by the sofabed which can be adjusted to a height convenient for reading in bed as well as for sitting on the sofa.

STUDY-DINING ROOMS

The study or den can also be an excellent room for dining in, especially if you have a round table in the middle of the room. This can happily serve as both library table, stacked with books and magazines, and a dining table. Similarly, a desk can, when necessary, be turned into a sideboard or serving table. A deep breakfront bookcase with cupboards underneath can also be used for serving, and the cupboards can hold china, glass and linens as well as files and papers. All lights should be on dimmer switches so that you can have, on the one hand, excellent work light and, on the other,

LEFT: This triangular space has been enhanced by being turned into an interesting work area. The sturdy bookshelves surrounding the desk help to balance the outsize window, and the warm terracotta tiles and oriental rugs complement the tones of the wood.

soft, background light which will mix sympathetically with candle-light for dining.

Bookshelves can literally line the walls, framing any sofa or sofabed as well as windows and doors. This will give you a strong sense of perspective, for the eye is automatically drawn to the view beyond a window or door, features emphasized by the depth of the bookshelves. The shelves themselves do not have to be made in particularly expensive woods, for timber can be stained or grained to look like mahogany, oak or walnut. You could also paint the shelves either to match dark walls, or in a contrasting colour like white. If you do paint shelves, make sure it is with a semi-gloss, satin or gloss finish so they can be easily wiped clean.

In the eighteenth and nineteenth centuries the edges of bookshelves were often finished with leather or buckram fringes which automatically dusted the books as they were withdrawn from the shelf. This seems to be an idea eminently worth reviving since a fringe in any material also looks decorative and softens the dominant horizontals.

Shelving units can be bought in a wide range of finishes, from wood to lacquer and melamine to glass, and in a stunning variety of permutations to fit any space. They come complete with drop-leaf desks, bar refrigerators, housing for a variety of home electronic equipment and tailor-made space for books, tapes, files and discs. Many of these units include beds which fold away behind neat doors, as well as full-length cupboards, and most can be fully closed up so that where one moment there is a fully functional work space, the next there is just a panelled wall or walls.

Workroom Tips

✔ Avoid a high contrast in light between a work surface and computer screen and the rest of the room. All general lighting should be controlled by dimmer switches and natural light through windows by slotted shades or blinds.

✔ Buy the best and most capacious desks and file units that you can. Nothing is more infuriating than not having enough surface space for a project you are working on, or struggling with drawers that stick and jam.

✔ Try to have everything you could possibly need immediately to hand. U-and L-shaped work areas are ideal, especially when combined with a swivel chair on castors.

87

KITCHENS

There are, of course, many different ways to design kitchens. It all depends upon your personal taste, lifestyle and budget, on factors like space and climate and on whether you are able to start from scratch or are trying to improve an existing room. Basically, however, most kitchen designs fall into three main categories:

•The kitchen as a workroom. In my experience, however sleek and efficiently planned, however state-of-the-art the equipment, this generally ends up as a passageway between the refrigerator, the coffee maker and the microwave.

•The kitchen as a necessity. A room where meals have to be produced and, if the space permits, are often eaten, though generally on the run. A kitchen, in fact, which is used more as a family refuelling station than as anything else.

•The kitchen as a family room. A heart-of-the-home place where the act of cooking is enjoyed, where family and other meals are eaten and where people tend to congregate for pleasure, chat and sometimes joint culinary effort.

I confess, my own tastes tend decidedly toward the last category, for I love both to cook and to eat in kitchens. But I find that

RIGHT: This homely kitchen – with its beams and waxed brick floor, dried herbs and flowers, cheerful plants and generous work surfaces – has a pleasant eating area under the window.

BELOW: A basically white kitchen is made warmer by the use of old wooden dressers, cupboards and chairs.

there is a curious anomaly about kitchen usage in the late twentieth century. For despite the facts that kitchen appliances, cabinets, units and utensils have reached unprecedented heights of sophistication;that a 'good' kitchen is supposed to be one of the best selling points of a house; that cookery books sell in the millions – despite all this, convenience foods and catering services have never ever been in such demand and, according to various polls, large numbers of people now know nothing at all about cooking. Much of the explanation for this is probably that, in the increasing numbers of households where both partners work, there is of course less time for cooking. None the less, most people still like to have the possibility of being able to cook quickly and efficiently and like to plan their kitchens accordingly.

DESIGNING KITCHENS FROM SCRATCH

Being able to design your kitchen from scratch is an enviable opportunity. Once you have decided what type of kitchen you want and where and how you want to site it – depending, of course, on your budget – you can start to plan the space. Most kitchen cabinet suppliers will plan kitchens; alternatively, you might decide to have custom-built units. Whatever you choose, it is still a useful exercise to find out what works best and, most importantly, what works best for you.

Professional kitchen-planners, given a well-proportioned space, will form a design based on the sequence of operations known as the 'work triangle' which comprises the different areas for food preparation, cooking and clearing up. Clearly, the dimensions and positioning of the work triangle

will be determined by your space. Although each area should have enough space allotted to it to work efficiently, it should not be placed too far apart from the others. If you analyse it, you can do an awful lot of walking back and forth between refrigerator, sink, dishwasher, work surfaces, hob and oven in the course of preparing and clearing up a meal.

In fact, small kitchens, where most things are immediately to hand, often work more efficiently, contrary to expectations, than large ones. So if you do have the bonus of a large kitchen space to work with, keep the actual work area within it compact. Each side of the work triangle should measure no more than 1.2 to 2.1 m (4 to 7 ft); the rest of the space should be left for storage (which you can *never* have too much of) and extras such as a large, scrubbable (or at least wipeable) table, chairs, a dresser and, if you still have room, even an armchair or sofa. It is worth remembering also that one of the most comforting items in an eat-in kitchen can be a fireplace, so make room for one, if it is at all possible to do so.

Planning good kitchens means making sure that the workflow is as streamlined as possible. You should therefore organize the storage around each work area according to your needs. For example, sharp knives, chopping boards, basins and whisks should be by the preparation area; wooden spoons, cooking tools and utensils near the stove; herbs, spices, seasonings and condiments in between preparation and cooking areas; coffee near the coffee maker, tea near the kettle and so on.

You will also need to think about the number and type of appliances you are going to have and their exact position, so that

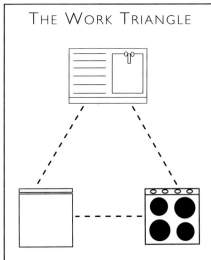

THE WORK TRIANGLE

A classic kitchen work triangle of refrigerator, oven and sink area placed sufficiently close to save tiring leg work but far apart enough to avoid crowding. The ideal distance between appliances should be no more than 1.2 to 2.1 m (4 to 7 ft), and the total triangle no more than 6.6 m (22 ft).

TOP RIGHT: Tall, old-fashioned cabinets have been sponge-painted in with the walls in a splendidly spacious kitchen (as can be judged by the length of the refectory table). The kitchen units look superimposed on to the room rather than built in. The lighting is amusingly idiosyncratic.

BOTTOM RIGHT: Kitchen units are clad in the same tongue-and-groove wood as the ceiling, giving the space a strong sense of unity.

Adding Storage

Even if you think you cannot possibly squeeze any more storage into a room that really seems to need more, there are often further ways to extend the available space.

✔ Look up. Saucepan racks suspended from the ceiling will allow you to free up a lot of space formerly occupied by saucepans, sieves and colanders. And you can also add hanging vegetable baskets, bunches of herbs and onions.

✔ Is there space to put things between the tops of cabinets and the ceiling? This is often a good place for casseroles, serving dishes, pots and pans that you do not use very much.

✔ Cup hooks fixed along the undersides of cabinets or shelves will take a good many mugs, cups, and jugs as well as cooking tools.

✔ Wire baskets fixed underneath shelves will give additional storage, as will slim shelves fixed to the backs of closet or cupboard doors.

✔ Plastic-coated wire grids, pieces of peg board, or wooden slats, make a good base for a number of cooking tools, measures, and so on which can be hung from S hooks, again freeing up drawer space.

✔ You might be able to add a butcher block stand on wheels with shelves and a wire basket underneath which will provide both extra work and storage space wherever needed.

✔ Don't forget about the exposed sides of end base and wall-hung cabinets. You could probably add extra shelves here.

you can site enough electrical outlets for comfort and safety. If you are planning a kitchen from scratch and cannot afford a dishwasher, a sophisticated hob or double oven right away, you should still allow for them in the future. You can always disguise the holes left for them, for example, by curtaining off the gap for a dishwasher, or having a wooden chopping board fitted over the space to be filled later by a hob. All this may sound like simple common sense, but in the rush and confusion of the planning process these things can easily be overlooked.

THE ESSENTIAL WORK PLAN

Even if you are going to employ professional kitchen planners you will still need to show them a sketch plan of the room you envisage (for instructions, see p. 24). If you are planning the room yourself, it is essential to measure

ABOVE: Clean-cut white units and appliances in this London river home are warmed by the wooden floor, the counter tops and the gentle curves of the arches.

RIGHT: Even without kitchen cabinets this rustic but handsome room is nevertheless a good working kitchen with plenty of countertop space as well as generous shelving and durable surfaces.

everything with the utmost accuracy, for in a kitchen, especially one with not much space to spare, a single wrong measurement can be disastrous. You must also mark in the position of pipes, awkward breaks in the wall, low windows, any existing electrical outlets and any other permanent features, such as doors, heating or air conditioning grilles, ducts, and skirting or base boards.

Ask yourself questions about the best way to organize the space. Would one arrangement of your working triangle be better for you than another? Could the distance between the refrigerator and the sink area be lessened by adding an island unit to the centre of the room? Would a free-standing, free-moving butcher block work-surface on wheels be the answer? For inspiration, find examples of good working arrangements in magazines and brochures.

KITCHEN LIGHT

As in most rooms you will need both general, or ambient, light, and work light (for food preparation, cooking, washing up). If the room is also used for eating, you can add accent light (candles, oil lamps) to show off any decorative objects or textures.

If you are designing a room from scratch, it is useful to install recessed downlights and wall-washers for maximum flexibility of lighting; they can be judiciously angled on worktop and sinks to provide general and accent light as well as work light. If, however, recessed light is difficult for any reason, try neat tracks with small spots which also provide considerable flexibility; these can be run from former central ceiling outlets.

If you want overhead light over a table, you could use a rise-and-fall fixture or an attractive old light as a counterpoint to the more clinical general lighting. Over-counter light can be provided, or boosted, by tubular lights fixed under cabinets and concealed by a pelmet of some sort. Fluorescent tubes last the longest and often give more light per watt, but try to find the warm white or ultra blue varieties that make food look particularly good.

Whatever kind of light you have, try and insist on having a dimmer switch. You can use dimmers to regulate the intensity of the light and, if you eat in the

Track lighting over the sink and counter tops gives good working light by night and boosts daylight, helpful even though one wall is entirely composed of window.

kitchen, hide the kitchen clutter as well as making the dining table more of a separate area.

If you have a little desk area in the kitchen, make sure that you have a small desk lamp or a wall light fixed just over the surface to cast light down on it for easy reading of recipes and any writing you want to do.

IMPROVING EXISTING KITCHENS

When you really set your mind to it, almost all existing kitchens can be improved, often at not too much expense. A surprising number of grouses about kitchens centre around a lack of storage and a lack of style. As it happens, it takes a good deal of ingenuity to infiltrate extra storage into a small space, but it is often surprisingly easy to inject more style and to improve a kitchen's looks. By simply repainting existing cabinets and retiling work surfaces you can transform a drab kitchen into an attractive room. New window and floor treatments can also make a huge difference.

MORE WORK SPACE

Some or all of the above methods might also supply you with more work space. Be ruthless and get rid of anything hanging around that you cannot remember using or having a need for in the last six months. Otherwise, try covering a sink with a made to measure chopping board or turning top drawers into work tops. This can be done by fitting them to a slim block of wood, the same width as the drawer, so that it can slide in and out of the unit, balancing on top of the relevant drawer when it is pulled out. In a galley kitchen a panel attached to an end wall can be flipped up to rest on the opposite wall surface when needed.

Cheap Ideas for Cosmetic Improvements

✔ Paint over shabby or unfortunately coloured tiles with gloss paint. Brighten tile walls with a contrasting coloured grout, or give a run of tiles a border.

✔ Try painting *all* the surfaces white in eggshell and satin finish, including the floor (covered with a couple of coats of polyurethane). Add colour with stencils, wallpaper borders or *découpage*, as well as new accessories, like brightly coloured tea towels, storage jars, plants and a shelf of cookbooks.

✔ Strip old cabinets down to the original wood and re-paint them with an interesting *faux* finish.

✔ Put new glass doors and false mullions on cabinet doors above work surfaces or take doors off altogether to reveal open shelves.

✔ Change window treatments. Take down old blinds or curtains and put up glass or wooden shelves instead to let in the light. Paint the window surround a contrast colour to the wall and add half-length curtains in a fresh, light fabric.

✔ Cheer up old counter tops by covering them with contact paper given a couple of coats of hardening polyurethane: it works like a dream.

✔ Cover old walls with new panelling or tongue-in-groove boarding fixed vertically, horizontally, or on the diagonal.

✔ Strip away old plaster to reveal the brick wall underneath.

95

KITCHEN MAKEOVER – BEFORE AND AFTER

The obvious advantage of this kitchen is its size which allows it easily to accommodate an eating area at one end. It was, however, dingy and neglected looking – in obvious need of freshening up! The main criterion in renovating this space was to make it efficient for a working couple with little time for weekday shopping. A large fridge/freezer has therefore been installed, together with a new dishwasher and a practical double oven. The expense of these new appliances, however, meant that little was left in the budget to buy new units. These have therefore been painted and given attractive hinges and handles, and they do not look at all out of place with the new tiles and wallpaper border.

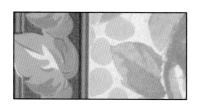

The subtly coloured floral wallpaper border tempers and softens the cool whites of the newly-painted kitchen.

This small-scale fruit-patterned wallpaper creates a pretty, country effect in the eating area.

The cupboards in the kitchen have all been lined with an attractive rose-mottled shelf paper that matches the wallpaper border and splashback tiles.

DINING ROOMS

When rooms are in short supply, single-purpose dining rooms are something of a luxury. More often than not, dining rooms have to double as libraries, studies or occasional guest rooms. In the same way, halls, kitchens and porches can become places to eat, or a living room might have a small alcove at one end suitable for use as a dining area.

In fact, although a proper dining room seems such a traditional feature of a home, rooms intended solely for dining did not become the norm until the late eighteenth century. Until that time, tables for eating at were set up in any convenient area, which explains why dining tables dating from before the nineteenth century are comparatively rare in comparison with the profusion of nineteenth-century drop-leaf tables so readily available from antique shops.

So, although it is very pleasant to have a separate dining room, its absence need not be too much of a disappointment. Moreover, any well-dressed and gently lit table is apt to become a kind of island,

LEFT: This is a somewhat mysterious room of squares and rectangles, the dominating paintings made to seem even more prominent by the dark walls. The square table with its inlaid panels and the herringbone lozenges of the parquet floor heighten the effect. Recessed halogen spots give dramatic light, boosting, when needed, the softer light of the candles.

RIGHT: The intense colour of the fruit and vegetable patterned tablecloth in an otherwise all blue and white room throws the table and old panelled benches into vivid relief. This exotic 'island' is set against the calm of the room and the dreamy landscape outside.

whatever its surroundings, so long as the food and company are both enjoyable!

Separate dining rooms do, however, offer all kinds of opportunities for fantasy and splendour – a stage setting for the act of dining and celebration.

If the room is to be used for lunching as well as dining, it could be decorated in soft, pale colours which will look equally good in daylight and by candlelight. If, however, the room is mostly used at night, warm, rich colours – ranging from dark red, green, blue, nutmeg and chestnut to soft rose, apricot, ginger, terracotta and marmalade – provide a splendid background for gilt, silver, glass, flowers, firelight, oil-lamp- light and candles.

Walls can be papered, painted, hung with fabric or panelled, and, wherever possible, mirrors should be placed to reflect the light. Carpeted floors are luxurious in dining rooms, but you should guard against food and drink stains, as well as the damage caused by the dragging of chairs.

As well as a table and chairs, dining rooms need reasonably

generous serving and storage areas. But do not worry if the space is rather small, as long as you have room to seat eight comfortably, for most dining rooms benefit from a feeling of intimacy. Even if you are designing a traditional room, it does not matter if you cannot find or afford a traditional mahogany or other polished wood table. You can use any old table (though a round or oval top on a secure base is easier for companionable parties) covered with a floor-length cloth in some matching or contrasting fabric and topped with a scarf-shaped over-cloth that can be laundered easily. It is really much better to spend any spare money on good-looking and *comfortable* chairs. Nothing is less conducive to the enjoyment of even the best food and company than frail, rickety, or over-hard seating, however elegant or stylish it may look.

LIGHTING

Undoubtedly, candlelight – from chandeliers and wall sconces as well as from candlesticks – gives the gentlest light in a dining room. However, it is very important to keep a watch on any naked flame and to extinguish all candles at the end of the meal. Electric light is safer but can cast a too harsh light unless attached to a dimmer switch. Uplights in corners can provide ambient light, and serving areas need a light which can be switched off or dimmed right down after use.

DUAL-PURPOSE DINING ROOMS

Most people are in the position of having to turn other rooms temporarily into dining rooms. Although brought about by necessity, the resulting hybrid rooms can really be very attractive. The nicest kind of formal dual-purpose room is the dining room /library or dining room/study. The nicest kind of informal dining room is the kitchen/dining room.

If you have the former the best kind of table is undoubtedly round. When you are not using the table for eating, it can be used as a library table piled with books, papers and magazines. Dining chairs may be dispersed around the room. Desks and bookshelves with a breakfront can be used for serving as well as for storing crockery, cutlery, glassware, and table linens, along with files, papers and other library /study miscellanea.

In a kitchen/dining room, the shape of table depends more on the shape of the room. But any table should be wipeable and, if wood, scrubbable so that it can be used for cooking preparation as well. Of course, if there is room, it is nice to have an old dresser, to show off china, pottery, glass, old kitchen utensils or whatever may be attractively displayed. Removable tie-on chair pillows or cushions can be covered in a fresh, cheerful-looking fabric to match or co-ordinate with tablecloth or napkins. The same lighting tips apply as for dining rooms that do not serve any secondary function.

Dining areas in living rooms benefit from long refectory or trestle tables that the family can use for many purposes when not dining. Drop-leaf tables are extremely practical if space is restricted.

Large blue and white diamond-shaped tiles echo the diamond window panes in this smoky-walled kitchen/dining room. The refectory table looks splendidly gregarious and the somewhat higgledy-piggledy shelves are crammed with glass, pottery, silver, pewter, cookbooks and other kitchen impedimenta.

100

Small black squares set into the corners of the floor tiles, a black Venetian blind and the black wheels of the mobile towel rack, though only small touches, make a strong contrast with the prevailing white in this sunny room.

BATHROOMS

As with kitchens, it is a rare luxury to get a chance to design a bathroom or bathrooms from scratch. Few of us even get the opportunity to renovate one, in the sense of replacing and re-sitting both fixtures and equipment.

Fortunately, it can be almost as much fun to revive old bathrooms cosmetically. Baths and basins can be resurfaced, old tiles, floors and walls replaced, and the effect of these relatively minor changes can be impressive. Even if bathroom expenditure is a long way down your list of priorities, these simple alterations – or others such as painting over ugly tiles, and small amounts of wallpapering and carpeting – can achieve disproportionately successful results.

There is now an enormous range of bathroom accessories of all shapes, sizes and types. In spite of the popularity of large whirlpool baths – as well as plunge tubs – there is an equal demand for old and reproduction enamel baths (and basins). If you do choose to replace a bath with an old-fashioned or reproduction version – or have an old bath resurfaced and want to update the taps and shower unit – there are some excellent reproductions of turn-of-the-century models to choose from. You can have hand-held showers in coated and uncoated brass finishes, as well as in chrome, and these can also be wall-mounted. Often, the taps have rounded white centres with 'H' and 'C' in black.

Various manufacturers are now producing floral and other prettily patterned bathroom equipment in matching sets. Whatever the style, all baths look good – if there is space – encased in wide-edged tile surrounds.

Large two-tone ochre diamond-laid tiles are echoed in the much smaller diamond design of the floor. Notice the claw feet of the old-fashioned bath.

If you have an existing pedestal wash basin with limited storage space, you can buy a slim rolling cart on wheels which simply rolls up beside the basin and can hold as much as a built-in unit under the sink. There are also neat units which come complete with their own mirror, built-in lighting and surrounding vertical storage, which will fit into the slimmest bathroom space.

If, on the other hand, you have a large space and several different members of a household sharing the bathroom, you would be well advised to install double basins – and double medicine cabinets. A double-arched mirrored cabinet unit, with recessed storage and double basins can look extremely elegant, especially when complemented by attractive rails.

Heated towel rails are usually available from stockists in classic brass, chrome and white enamel. They should, I would suggest, be installed in every bathroom, and particularly in those of old houses that are large and susceptible to draughts.

TILES AND OTHER FINISHES

Just as for bath fixtures, there is now a great demand for – and range of – period-style tiles, tiling details and borders. It is now possible to turn your bathroom into a room as elegant and opulent as the grandest and most lavish Edwardian hotel bathroom. There are quite literally hundreds of tiles and tiled borders to choose from in almost every good tile shop, and, given some imagination, you can easily make your own designs by arranging patterned or plain-coloured tiles in interesting configurations – either geometrically repeating or 'arbitrarily' juxtaposed. In fact, tiles in general are now so sophisticated that, given

Dramatically dark floral wallpaper in this interesting bathroom is all but covered by a gallery of framed prints and drawings. The bird's-eye maple-framed photographs mounted over the marble basin form a contrasting frieze.

the available finance, it would be difficult *not* to produce streamlined bathrooms, especially since the majority of designs are now also available in matching non-slip floor tiles.

Marble tiles and slabs are a somewhat expensive alternative to tiles, but they can help to make enviably handsome bathrooms, especially if used to face floors, bath surrounds, walls, basins and shower units.

If you like the richness of mahogany in a bathroom – but are concerned about the environment and want to try to avoid using hard woods – you can stain unfinished wood units very successfully and achieve much the same effect for a fraction of the price. (Make sure, however, that you seal and varnish them or they will be very easily marked from watersplashes.)

LEFT: Dark blue mosaic tiles completely line walls and floor in this room with its shiny chrome fittings. The only concession to softness is the plentiful supply of white towels.

ABOVE: Unglazed Mexican tiles on the counter-top and solid, plain wooden mirror frames give a pleasingly earthy quality to this bathroom. Cane chairs and plants add interesting contrast.

Comforting Accessories

✔ Heated towel rails have been in use for so long in Britain that it is surprising they have not been more prevalent across the Atlantic. Now, however, there are a good many types to choose from, any of which should be a wise investment given their practicality in keeping towels warm and dry.

✔ It is possible to create striking effects with small details, such as plants, towels, prints, paintings, and accessories..

✔ Even if bathroom expenditure is way down on your list of priorities, you can still paint over ugly tiles and, remembering to use polyurethane, achieve a quick cover-up with wallpaper (or paint with a wallpaper border).

105

BEDROOMS

In theory, bedrooms should be the easiest rooms to design. Not only do they have a definite main function, but they are also personal rooms in which you should be able to please yourself.

In practice, of course, bedrooms often have to be multi-functional – to suit a partner or a different situation, or to incorporate a home office. Guest rooms too, although not personal, need to be made as interesting and comfortable as possible if they are not to look like chain hotel rooms. So, all in all, bedroom planning has to be thought through quite carefully.

GENERAL PLANNING
In an ideal world a bedroom would be large enough to hold as big and comfortable a bed as desired. There would be room, without its looking cluttered, for capacious bedside tables accommodating books, glasses and bottled water, flowers, tall lamps (if there are no swing arm wall lamps), magazines, a clock, a

ABOVE: Ceiling beams and floorboards are much the same reddish brown, and form a strong frame for the bed with its colourful quilt, dazzling white pillows, valance and neighbouring tablecloth.

LEFT: The similar tones of the polished, gilded and inlaid bedhead and the rich paisley bedspread contrast with the beautifully worked white sheet and pillow cases.

radio, a telephone and notebooks. There would also be a chest of drawers, armchairs and a comfortable chaise-longue (all with good reading light); a chest for blankets, duvet or comforter and extra pillows; a TV and VCR set at a good angle for the bed; a well-lit dressing table; a desk and comfortable desk chair; roomy walk-in cupboards; and an exercise area with a view of the television which could be screened or shut off when not in use. There would definitely be a fireplace and, of course, an en-suite bathroom.

Since the world is not ideal, one seldom finds a room with such capacity. More often than not, once the bed is chosen and in place, the rest of one's design ingenuity is spent trying to squeeze in as many bare necessities as possible without the space appearing hopelessly cramped.

ILLUSIONS OF SPACE
The best way to give the illusion of space when there is not much actual square footage, is to avoid clutter. Keep as large an area of

RIGHT: A nineteenth-century sleigh bed fits neatly into the window alcove lined with bookshelves in this pine-panelled room. The solidity of the wood and the polished hexagonal terracotta floor tiles is counterbalanced by the tied-back white voile curtains.

ABOVE: An idiosyncratic bedroom with a high ceiling and small windows becomes a thoroughly comfortable room for general living with a large fireplace flanked by Victorian armchairs and other useful pieces of furniture, including, of course, a sleigh bed.

Bow-decorated *couronnes* form pretty
backings for a neat pair of sleigh beds
with identical paisley throws laid over
the footboards. The side-table and the
curved back of the Victorian chair echo
the undulating lines of the beds.

floor showing as is practical. Built-in cupboards – or pre-fabricated units that look as though they have been built in – obviously help, especially if the doors can be decorated in keeping with the walls, or mirrored. You can 'lose' the bulk of cupboards if you actually construct them around the bed so that the bed appears to be recessed in a convenient alcove. Failing that, you could buy quite an inexpensive but handsome old armoire or wardrobe (providing that there is enough room for one, remembering that you have to get it up the stairs and through the door). If space is really tight, you can bring in cloakroom racks and conceal them with curtains or ever-useful screens.

PLACING THE BED

Careful positioning of the bed can often maximize the apparent space in a room, so long as you always allow for some sort of convenient bedside table or shelves. Beds placed in corners certainly make the left-over floor area seem bigger, and beds placed in the centre of a room can be dramatic. In a small room, if windows are well fitted and not draughty, you can place the bed against the window, using curtains as a backdrop. In a larger room, you can even place the bed between the windows as opposed to the more conventional position against the facing wall.

A single room – or room for a single occupant – can be made to seem more like a personal sitting room if you use a sofabed, studio couch or day bed (with two ends) rather than a conventional bed. If you do not want the bother of pulling the mattress out at night and putting it away in the morning, you can set it longways against a wall. Alternatively, you could use a fold-away bed concealed in an apparently panelled cupboard or wall.

If you have two single beds in a room that you want to make more like a sitting-room, try placing them at right angles with a large table in between and throwing attractive covers over them during the day.

GUEST ROOMS

Proper guest bedrooms (as opposed to rooms with sofabeds for guests in them) should emphasize the inviting qualities of the bed itself. This can be made to look as grand, splendid or exotic as you wish and, if you work imaginatively with fabrics, need not be too expensive.

The bed should be reasonably firm (many people prefer a hard bed for their back). You can, however, improve an uncomfortable mattress by placing another on top of it. One does not always know one's guests' sleeping habits, so it is best to play safe and supply them with two firm and two soft pillows, remembering that some people are allergic to feathers.

Guest bedrooms should always have, if possible: a writing table or a desk; a comfortable armchair; plenty of good books and magazines; bottled water and glasses; fresh flowers or plants and, maybe, a bowl of fruit. In winter, a real fire blazing in the fireplace is the ultimate luxury.

For a guest bathroom you might consider supplying towelling robes, toothpaste, toothbrushes, combs, razors, a sewing kit and a hair dryer.

If the furniture in the guest room is made up of quite disparate odds and ends, you can make them look more of a piece, either by painting or lacquering them the same colour, or by covering them with the same fabric.

Alternative Storage

✔ If you buy a bed that is fairly high off the ground you can use the space beneath the bed frame to harbour suitcases and other large objects. You could also buy storage drawers made especially for under-bed space.

✔ Shelves built around the top of a bed may be used for books and general display as well as acting as a kind of extended bedhead. Low shelves at the foot of a bed can be double-sided and hold a TV, stereo, books, magazines, files and other useful objects..

✔ Chests of drawers on either side of the bed can double as bedside tables, and drop-leaf desks with drawers can come in handy, when additional clothes storage is required..

MASTER BEDROOM MAKEOVER – BEFORE AND AFTER

The bare bones of this master bedroom show it to be neither a particularly large or distinguished room, with no architectural details nor any real charm. In decorating this space, the aim was to make it suitable for a young couple: light, airy and pretty, without being overly flouncy.

In its finished state, the bed becomes the central feature under a canopy from which hang filmy four-poster-like curtain (see p.65). Blue voile is an inexpensive material with which you can acheive a luxurious effect. Paper and fabrics in co-ordinating Indian designs cover the walls and bed, and a neat border from the same collection is used to define the space between walls and the ceiling.

This pleasantly striped fabric covers the queen-size bedhead as well as forming the valance (or dust ruffs).

A larger-scale patterned fabric is used for the comfortably quilted custom-made bedspread and for the pillows.

The colours of this wallpaper exactly match those of the fabric used for the bedspread. Both designs were adapted from Indian fabric documents.

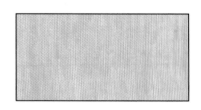

Airy pale blue voile forms the bed curtains and overhead valance. These are fixed with Velcro to a slim wooden frame mounted on to the ceiling directly over the bed.

110

CHILDREN'S ROOMS

I am a firm believer in trying to create rooms for children that will grow with them. I am certainly not against fantasy (some of the children's furniture and accessories available are very beguiling), but I do think the framework of any child's room should be strictly pragmatic. That is to say that since, presumably, you will not want to change the main components of the room, these should be chosen for long-term durability. I like to think that the rooms I design will stay basically the same, with only minor changes, from infancy to late adolescence.

WIRING FOR CHILDREN

Before you think about the decorating and furnishing, make sure that the existing wiring is entirely safe, and flexible enough to last the course of the growing child's tenure. If you are rewiring the room from scratch, site all outlets above a toddler's reach. If the existing wiring has been checked and proved to be safe, you should try to have outlets shuttered as far as possible.

General lighting and any lamps in the room should be worked by dimmer switches. You will also need good task lighting for all stages of the child's life, as well as adequate power – for TV, stereo, and, later, perhaps, a computer.

This means, that, apart from any ceiling and wall lights, there should be outlets next to the position in which the bed will be placed, and several outlets by the play/work-surface area. It is not always possible to foresee where furniture is going to be placed over the years, so you should allow for flexibility by installing double outlets in all four corners and in the centre of each wall.

FURNITURE TO LAST

I always install one indispensable item: a run of chests of drawers, with (depending on the room size) one or two knee-holes. On top of the chests I put a continuous worktop which can be made of polyurethaned wooden or laminated board and is therefore easy to wipe clean.

This simple unit will, under various guises, be very useful for years. The top can be used for changing nappies and holding toys, the drawers used for clothes and other equipment. As the child grows older, the top can be used for play and homework, for TV, stereo, computer, typewriter and anything else the child or teenager wants to put on it.

Such a unit can be painted, repainted or stencilled and will certainly perform many functions without becoming dated. It can remain while a cradle gives way to a cot, and the cot to bunk beds (to accommodate a sibling or a friend) and the bunk beds are dismantled and turned into useful sofabeds.

Ideally a child's room should have a built-in cupboard, with the rail at waist-height for easy access for children. If not, there should be at least some sort of securely fastened free-standing cupboard. The only other furniture you will actually *need* in the room will be one or two desk chairs, depending upon space, and perhaps a rocking chair or armchair. You could also add a chest to hold extra playthings when the child is young. Later it can be painted, lacquered or covered and recycled as a low bedside table between the beds.

Another useful piece of furniture is a sturdy cart or trolley. This can hold all the infant impedimenta which can be conveniently drawn up close to a nursing mother. (Be careful, however, when the child starts to walk: it should not be used by a toddler as a walker trainer or plaything.) Later it can house a TV, stereo, tapes and discs, and when it is no longer wanted, can be recycled to the kitchen.

Once these basic pieces of furniture are allowed for in the budget (all can be bought in an unfinished state and finished as you like), the only other essential purchases over the years are window treatments, bed clothes and coverings, and, possibly, new rugs.

Walls can be plain painted, so that they are easily wiped or washed and finished off with decorative paper border, or stick-on, easy-to-peel-off motifs. Another approach is to have a painted dado up to adult waist-height which can be wiped clean of finger marks and scribbles, leaving the upper part of the walls to be papered more decoratively. You could always start off papering the walls with washable vinyl in whatever colourway or design you like, remembering that it will have to act as a good background to all the other objects that will inevitably be superimposed.

A practical and fun solution to the problem of children marking and scribbling on walls and doors is to spray certain areas with a couple of coats of blackboard paint. With luck, your child or children will understand that they can use this surface as often as they like, but that all other surfaces in the home are sacrosanct.

Whatever style of decoration yu choose, do remember that the room must ultimately be both practical and convivial to the child. Even in a small space, it is possible to create a stimulating environment suitable for learning activities and games, in which they should be free to create their own world of the imagination.

TOP: Attic rooms almost always make great spaces for kids and this is no exception. The blue floor and white walls and curtains make a good background for the riot of colour in the toys and furniture.

BOTTOM: This soaring space with its huge windows and supporting beams has to be a child's paradise. The space has been cleverly divided by the shelving unit and the ropes, pulleys and full-size slide, making suitable areas in which to eat, play, relax and sleep. The rope net, which divides the bed from the rest of the room, is, of course, great for climbing.

BELOW: Bunk beds are as useful for playing or lounging on as they are for sleeping in.

ABOVE: The Roman blind (or shade) with yellow check bows picks up the colours of the room.

The blind (or shade) is of a fresh checked and striped cotton that matches well with the ceiling and wallpaper.

This crayon-scribble wallpaper is printed in soft multi-colours and provides an attractive textural background for prints and posters.

CHILDREN'S ROOM MAKEOVER – STAGE 1

As long as the furniture is well chosen, it is perfectly possible to keep much the same furnishings in a child's room from infancy to adolescence, so that only cosmetic alterations are necessary over the years. You can get by with really surprisingly little change and still cater generously for each age group.

The arrangement in this room allows for an extra child or, if necessary, space for friends sleeping over.

The sturdy furniture in this room includes bunk beds, three chests of drawers, a cupboard with a changing-tray top, a trolley, and a long melamine-covered top to turn two of the chests into a work-play surface. To this are added two chairs, a rocking chair and some shelves supported by brackets. All these furnishings have been painted blue and white and they are complemented by a matching carpet.

This delicate blue and white wallpaper has a bird and cloud motif making it highly appropriate for use on the ceiling of the room.

The strong, clear blue of the painted furniture creates the key colour note with which all other elements must harmonize.

ABOVE: The white surface stretched across the chests of drawers creates a desk/playtop: note that a child may need a cushion on the chair. The pinboard is both practical and fun to use.

BELOW: Variegated cushions on the sofabeds make this sleeping/sitting/lounging corner very attractive. The space between the beds has been filled by a large parson's table painted white.

ABOVE: On the parson's table are a number of fun and practical objects: a table lamp and books; a sculpted bust and wooden whale; a clock, television and telephone. The bed and cushion covers are easily washable.

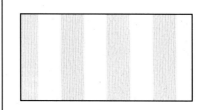

The striped yellow and white wallpaper is used in conjunction with a chair rail to form a neat dado.

The denim of the cushion draws attention to the other complementary blues ranged around the room.

CHILDREN'S ROOM MAKEOVER – STAGE 2

Now that the child is older the room has undergone a major cosmetic change, although the basic furnishings remain the same. Polystyrene chair rails make the walls more interesting; the area above has been painted plain yellow with a yellow striped paper beneath. The checked and striped Roman blinds have been replaced by apricot mini-blinds, and the carpet has been taken up to be used elsewhere. Sisal matting, which is tough and looks more up-to-date, has taken its place. The bunk beds have been painted white and turned into sofabeds at right angles to each other; the old cart and toy chest have been moved to the kitchen and the porch. Although the room now looks much altered with its teenage posters, added shelving and different floor covering, in fact very few of the basics have changed.

117

Peachy apricot sofabed covers have been quilted to give them extra warmth and shape. They are of plain cotton and easily washable.

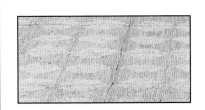

Pale cream sisal matting offers a practical and attractive neutral base for the orange and peach tones of the room.

ABOVE: The worktop now sports a computer and a desk lamp, as well as electric hair curlers and make-up. The original pinboard has given way to a much larger, more practical one.

CARING FOR YOUR
home

O nce you have decorated and furnished your home you will need to maintain it carefully, both to preserve your investment and for your own comfort. Many of your original decisions will have been taken with wider issues at stake than just the question of your budget and your choice of styles and colours. These issues concern the safety of yourself and your household and the maintenance of the fabric of the house or building, as well as the security of your possessions and the longevity of your new decorations.

When undertaking any new building work, it is your responsibility to comply with all building regulations. These relate to the general safety of, for example, wiring and plumbing, as well as to specific fire precautions, such as escape routes and internal doors. It is up to you to give notice to the local authority and to apply for housing inspection once the work is in progress. Any reputable builder or contractor should be familiar with the requirements and carry out the work to the proper safety standards.

You should also, at an early stage, think about what conditions might be insisted upon by your insurance company. They may require you to put in a burglar or fire alarm or some forms of protection that would be difficult and costly to install once your decorations are in place. You should consider all these questions now, remembering that safety must extend to the environment as well as to your household and your home.

LEFT AND RIGHT: Ceramics, metals, furniture and wooden objects of all sorts need special care and attention to keep them in good condition, and due consideration should be given to the way in which they are handled, stored or displayed.

This chapter then is devoted to *wise* decorating in every sense – to making sure that structural alterations are safe in the short, as well as the long term; to the best ways of securing your home; to preserving your improvements and to extending the life-span of your newly decorated rooms. It also covers the basic care of antiques. Although it is impossible to go into each of these topics in any depth, I want to give some pointers on a few of the more important aspects of caring for your home, which should be considered from the earliest planning stage.

SAFETY IN RENOVATION AND DECORATION

There are safety regulations which apply to almost every aspect of a building, from the proper siting of gas pipes, electrical wiring, boilers or furnaces and water tanks, to the installation of efficient ventilation in internal bathrooms, boiler or furnace rooms and kitchens. These regulations vary from country to country and, in the United States, from state to state, but whatever type of building work you are undertaking, you must make sure to observe them. You should quite easily be able to obtain the details from your local government or town planning offices.

You also have a responsibility to ensure that all due precautions are taken in the course of your renovations. For example, before demolishing walls you must make absolutely sure that they are not load-bearing. If you tap the walls and they sound very solid, they almost certainly are load-bearing, but you should never rely on this simple test alone: always get expert advice before going ahead. Another essential safety precaution is to find out exactly where all electric cables and pipes are located in the walls before drilling or hammering into

them. It is important that you always wear appropriate protective clothing, especially when working with chemicals such as paint strippers, bleaches and spirits. Check all tools such as power drills, saws and blades before use, keep them well-maintained and only operate them with extreme caution. Also test all ladders for safety before putting your weight on them.

Accidents in the home happen all too often, but by thinking ahead there is much you can do to prevent them. Apart from the risks of falls caused by uneven floors and poor lighting, the greatest threats to safety are generally posed by fire, gas, electricity and water. So you should carefully consider all aspects of your home under these headings.

FIRE

Sometimes your insurance company will insist, as a condition of your policy, that you install all, or some of the following: a fire alarm, smoke detector, fire escape, hydrants, portable extinguishers and fire blankets. If they don't, you should, at the very least, have smoke detectors and portable extinguishers in the relevant places – beside the hob or oven, near fireplaces, in hallways and on landings. Your local fire station can make inspections of your residence and give advice if necessary. Check all escape routes that you might need in case of fire, especially from upper floors, and see that they are kept clear at all times. There should be no large, cumbersome objects blocking escape hatches in the attic roof or exits along corridors and so on. Ladders, fire doors and windows should be kept in constant good order and, since the electricity cuts out in a fire, always keep working torches in strategic places (by the master bed, in bathrooms and kitchens and by main doors).

GAS AND ELECTRICITY

It is essential to know how to turn off both systems at the main supply in case of emergency. Leaking gas can cause an explosion and electricity a fire. When moving into any new home it is of prime importance to have all wiring and gas lines checked, even if the house is new. Make sure all appliances conform to safety standards, ensure that you have them serviced regularly (even if nothing has gone wrong) and *always* read the manufacturer's instructions for their use.

If you are rewiring, make sure you have an adequate supply of sockets or outlets so that you do not have electric wires or cords trailing around. Never overload circuits. If you do not rewire and cannot add new outlets, make sure that you buy multi-outlet surge-suppressors to provide maximum outlets from one source safely. When leaving a home, remember to turn off all electrical appliances, especially the television, at the source.

WATER

As with electricity, you must check that all plumbing is in good condition. If you are moving into a new home this should be investigated immediately, as should the wiring. Leaking pipes, burst and dripping tanks and radiators, and broken gutters can all cause extensive damage to the fabric of the building. Make sure you know where the main water tap is and how to turn it off in an emergency. It is a good idea to label all main pipes, taps and stopcocks to remind yourself and others. The mixture of water and electricity is potentially lethal, so always switch off the mains electricity as well in the case of flooding. Never touch any electrical socket or appliance with wet hands.

Kitchens and utility rooms should be planned so that washing machines and dishwashers are sited in an area where overflowing machines cause least damage. Do not try to site a laundry room above a living or dining room, for example, and keep machines well away from carpets or matting.

Regular inspection should be made of all radiators (bleed them if necessary to expel air), gutters, pipes and drainage, as well as roofs. In very cold weather put plugs in basins and baths to prevent dripping water from freezing and make sure that all pipes in the attic are properly lagged.

Do not ignore the problems caused by damp in the home. Air must always be allowed to circulate, so make sure all rooms are well-ventilated or condensation and damp will cause damage. Timbers exposed to damp are liable to come under attack by mould and fungi – such as dry and wet rot which can be particularly insidious – so inspect them regularly. Walls in old houses are often susceptible to rising damp; once again the solution is to keep them as dry, warm and well-ventilated as possible or, if necessary, to seek expert attention.

SECURITY

The time to start thinking about security is before you begin your decorating. Burglar alarm systems, locks on doors, windows and skylights and security grilles and gates may well be insisted upon by your insurance company. Your local crime prevention officer will also usually be prepared to advise you and will sometimes arrange to come and inspect your home. So take any advice you can before you start decorating, as superimposed security systems can ruin your good work.

For insurance purposes, once your home is completed, it is wise to make a list of all the contents of your rooms, including appliances with their make and serial numbers, as well as furniture, furnishings, jewellery, valuables and clothes. Also, take photographs of valuable paintings, furniture and objects. This may sound pernickety, but it is incredibly easy to forget items in cases of major burglaries or fires.

Obviously, you should take all steps to prevent break-ins, including having good outside lighting and internal lights attached to time switches so they will go on and off when your house is empty. Do not close curtains in the daytime or let newspaper deliveries or letters pile up on the doorstep betraying the fact that your home is empty.

BEING SENSITIVE TO THE ENVIRONMENT

Remember that saving energy and natural resources is as good for the environment as it is for your bank balance. Thorough insulation, for example, will mean that you use – and pay for – less gas or electricity to heat your home. Attic walls and floors, outside walls, cylinders, water tanks and pipes should be well-insulated and lagged where appropriate. Heat can also escape through draughty doors, windows, floorboards and chimneys. Think about installing double-glazed windows and draught-proofing doors and fireplaces. Unused chimneys can be sealed off at the top (but do not block up a fireplace – which I would hate to do anyway – without fitting a ventilation grille in the chimney breast or flue to prevent condensation). Fitted carpets certainly warm up draughty floors, but once again do not block air vents or under-floor ventilation.

All central heating systems and boilers should be serviced regularly and thermostats checked. Try to make a conscious effort to be economical with electricity by using low-wattage bulbs, low-energy appliances and turning down thermostats whenever practicable. The same applies to water. Use dishwashers and washing machines sparingly and remember that showers use far less energy than baths. When buying any new electrical equipment compare its performance and energy-saving components with others. Find out about the pollutive qualities of fridges and freezers and avoid buying any that are clearly too big for your needs.

As a general rule, choose non-toxic and biodegradable cleaning products which are not damaging to the environment. Also try and cut down on the amount of waste your household generates and find out what recycling facilities are available to you locally.

PRESERVING YOUR IMPROVEMENTS

As soon as your home is finished you will have to take steps to ensure that you extend the lifetime of your new decorations and furnishings. Good housekeeping – whether it is done by you or by someone else – is an essential part of home maintenance. Basically, it consists of working out a system of regular dusting and cleaning; having plenty of storage space so you can keep things well ordered, tidy and clean; knowing how to arrange the home environment; and learning about the basic care of antiques to preserve them in the best possible condition.

Most housekeeping is a matter of common sense, mixed with some experience. Although it may sometimes seem like a chore, it is in fact a skill that will in the long run repay all the time and effort you put into it.

A REGULAR CLEANING ROUTINE

Some household jobs, such as vacuuming or dusting, need to be done at least twice a week, depending of course on where you live and how much use the rooms get. Other jobs, such as polishing or cleaning, can usually be done at less frequent intervals. Any schedule of cleaning should also include a regular room-by-room spring-clean of all its contents – from upholstery, rugs and carpets to window treatments, bookcases and lampshades. You should also make time for clearing out cupboards and shelves, and sorting through and checking little used items in storage.

Part of the practice of good housekeeping is, of course, knowing how to keep things clean. This means that you should be aware of the best way to hand wash, how to remove stains and when to take items to the dry-cleaners or call in professional help.

UPHOLSTERY

All upholstery needs regular vacuuming to prevent dust and dirt becoming ingrained and damaging to the fabric. It is always a good idea to have extra slip-covers made for the arms of chairs and sofas; these are the most vulnerable points of contact with dirty or greasy hands. Slip-covers can easily be removed and either washed or dry-cleaned, as appropriate, separately from the cover itself. Light or pale-coloured upholstery can be treated with a fabric-protector, such as Scotchguard, to repel stains and dirt.

Make sure that you can identify the different types of fabrics and surfaces in your home, and always follow manufacturers' instructions on how to care for them. Some materials can be successfully washed or shampooed (but test for colour fastness first); others need to be dry cleaned, sometimes by a specialist cleaner. Leather, plastic and vinyl surfaces can be washed with a warm, soapy, but not too wet, sponge or cloth

before being quickly dried. For tapestry, velvet and any fragile material, it is important to consult professional upholstery cleaners – and, in the case of antique materials, a textile conservator.

CARPETS AND RUGS

As with upholstery, regular cleaning of carpets and rugs is necessary to keep them in good condition. Trodden-in dirt can work its way into the pile of the carpet, causing minute cuts in the fibres. How often you vacuum depends, of course, on where the carpet or rug is laid, and what kind of rugs you have. In halls and corridors you will obviously need to vacuum more frequently than in a living room or bedroom which is less often used. Always use the correct setting on any vacuum cleaner – too high a setting on a fragile carpet can cause strands and frayed edges to be sucked into the machine. With a vulnerable Oriental or antique carpet, it is safer to brush it with a soft brush rather than risk vacuuming it – always take specialist advice on how to clean it.

Spills on a carpet should be mopped up promptly, using a dry cloth, paper towel or blotting paper to prevent the stain from spreading. You can then heap salt on to any remaining liquid and vacuum it off once it has dried. A light application of a vinegar and water solution is also sometimes effective on carpet stains. Be careful, however, if you use proprietary carpet cleaners as they can leave marks which are worse than the stain itself. Try removing candlewax by first scraping it off with a blunt knife. If more remains, put a piece of blotting or brown paper over the wax and go over it with a warm iron. If you have to remove chewing gum, press a polyurethane bag full of ice cubes against it until it hardens and can be easily peeled off.

PAINTWORK AND WALLS

Keep paintwork clean by regular dusting; it should also be washed occasionally with a mild detergent to remove marks and stains. Always wash from the top to the bottom or you will find that you leave drip marks on the wall.

Never use water on wallpaper unless it has been specially treated or is vinyl, in which case use nothing more than a damp cloth. Dirty marks can sometimes be gently rubbed off with an eraser or a piece of stale white bread. More stubborn stains and grease marks on fabric or wallpaper may respond to an application of moistened bicarbonate of soda or liquid dry cleaners. But, if in doubt, ask the advice of a professional, rather than experiment yourself.

FLOORS

Floors of any material – whether stone, wood, tile, vinyl or marble – need to be regularly swept, vacuumed or cleaned with a dry mop. They should be washed or scrubbed only when necessary, with a minimum amount of water and a mild detergent and dried carefully afterwards. Too much water can damage stone floors and cause the adhesive on tiled floors to lose its grip. Black marks made by rubber soles can be removed with a mixture of white spirit, water and detergent. Wooden, stone and marble floors can be polished very occasionally, and the shine buffed up with a clean cloth. If polished too often, polish and wax can easily build up and even darken the floor.

THE HOME ENVIRONMENT

Dirt, light, heat and humidity can all affect the condition of your furnishings and possessions. If unchecked, they can do great damage, particularly to antiques (see below). Too much sunlight is harmful to most organic materials –

wood, fabric, natural dyes and paper. Over time it can cause, for example, the edges of your curtains to fray, wooden furniture to discolour and pictures to fade. On a bright day you should therefore protect the contents of your home from direct sunlight by drawing the blinds or closing the shutters, if you have them.

An over-dry atmosphere can cause shrinkage and distortions in wood, paper and certain metals. Excessive humidity, on the other hand, can have serious effects on fabrics, books and furniture. It is important to try and adjust the environmental conditions of your home to avoid the fluctuations in temperature and humidity that do the most damage. If necessary, keep a humidifier on at the same time as the central heating, and keep damp walls and basements dry by using a low-output heater.

PESTS AND MOULDS

Wherever you live, it is difficult to avoid the nuisance of some form of pest – mice, silverfish, cockroaches, moths, ants and other insects. Woodworm is common in the form of the furniture beetle *anobium punctatum*, which bores into woodwork and weakens the joints of furniture. Moths can eat into clothes and carpets, and mice can gnaw into books and make their nest of materials they have shredded. Insect larvae tend to accumulate along the edge of skirting or base boards, behind furniture and along the cracks of floorboards, so regular vacuuming and cleaning of these areas is essential.

In all cases vigilance is called for, with inspections made around the home to forestall any damage. Prompt action to remove and isolate the infestation is important, but if you are unable to contain the problem yourself, you will have no

The silver among these objects should be sparingly cleaned with proprietary polishes; over-zealous polishing removes precious layers. Regular washing with warm, soapy water and thorough drying will prolong the shine on most objects.

choice but to call in fumigation or extermination experts.

Fungi in the form of moulds, wet and dry rots and mildew thrive in warm, damp conditions and can do great damage both to the fabric and contents of your home. Cellars, kitchens and bathrooms in particular will require good ventilation to avoid the problems of condensation. Be careful not to store objects in damp conditions, wrapped in polythene or sealed in boxes, and do not store or display anything against cold outside walls. If you discover any sign of damp or mould on the building itself, you should call in professional help. Most fungicides are poisonous and many damage certain materials, so do not attempt to use them yourself.

BASIC CARE OF ANTIQUES

All the general guidelines I have outlined above apply equally to the basic care of antiques. There are, however, some more specific measures you can take to ensure a long life for your most precious

possessions. Common sense, as always, plays the largest role, but preventive care must also take into account the different types of deterioration that can occur in different materials. Obviously, different categories of objects have diverse requirements, and it can be difficult to create an environment within a single home that is equally suitable for all materials. But don't be put off by the fact that you cannot re-create ideal museum conditions – it is possible to ensure that the basic conditions are sound and that your objects are in a relatively dry atmoshere, out of direct sunlight, well-supported and protected, and displayed where they will not be damaged by other objects. Don't be afraid to handle your antiques but, if they are fragile or prone to wear, do so judiciously and relatively seldom.

Once you are aware of the most suitable environmental conditions andthe best way of handling your antiques, you can often prevent the need for professional conservation and restoration. There will, nevertheless, always be cases where you will have to consult an expert. Never attempt any home repair which might damage an object, thereby diminishing its value.

WOODEN FURNITURE

Wood is the material most susceptible to changes in temperature and humidity. Exclusively dry conditions will cause it to shrink and crack, while damp conditions will cause it to swell and warp, which in turn will lead to any inlay or veneer rising or coming loose. So special care should always be given to the siting of furniture. Pieces should not be placed near sources of heat, like

Gilt mounts on this side-table need to be very carefully cleaned to avoid harming the surrounding wood. The fragile chairs on either side should always be moved with care.

fires or radiators; nor conversely, by a wall, on a damp floor or where they could suffer from condensation. The ideal situation is a well-ventilated room with a stable temperature, somewhere in the region of 18°C (64°F), and a constant relative humidity of 55%.

It is also important to protect old wood from exposure to light, both direct sunlight and spotlights and lamps. Some woods become bleached; others darken. Objects displayed or kept on top of pieces of furniture may leave scratch marks when they are moved across the surface, and water stains may occur from flower vases or *cache-pots*. Protect polished surfaces with brown felt and leather or glass mats under ornaments and move them around from time to time.

The polished surfaces of wooden furniture need regular and thorough dusting to keep them free of dirt and dust. This should be done with a clean, dry duster or chamois leather. Dusters should be shaken out and washed regularly and should be free of frayed edges or dangling threads which might catch on furniture or lift up pieces of veneer, inlay or moulding.

Contrary to general opinion, the less you polish the better. Polish does not *improve* wood, although it does give some protection and a generally gleaming appearance. The best wax polish is beeswax. As any wax or polish tends to build up on the surface, it should be applied only occasionally and very sparingly. Be careful how you use proprietary cleaners and special furniture creams as they may by harmful to some surfaces.

As a general rule do not move or handle antique furniture any more than is absolutely necessary. Moving furniture can frequently weaken the joints and fixings on which each piece depends. Pushing

or pulling it across the floor, even if it has castors, puts a strain on the joints as well as running the risk of snagging on carpets and rugs. So always lift any furniture gently and enlist the help of a companion if you have to move anything larger than chairs. Before lifting antique furniture, make sure that all parts are sound, for feet and loose pieces of veneer or mouldings can be very easily lost or damaged. Incidentally, do be careful, or implore others to be careful, with vacuum cleaners, brooms and mops: it is all too easy for the legs and feet of the furniture to be knocked and damaged by careless cleaning.

Inspect furniture regularly for signs of woodworm, a routine that is particularly important if pieces are made of walnut, pine, beech, oak and ash. Eggs are laid in cracks and crevices and, once hatched, the grubs bore into the wood, weakening the timber. The signs to look out for are a mass of tiny holes in the

back or underside of the piece and little piles of wood dust on the surface of the wood or on the floor beneath. Woodworm should be treated immediately it is discovered. This can either be done by applying a liquid insecticide or by having the piece of furniture professionally fumigated. In some countries, proprietary liquid insecticides are banned, in which case you will have to go to a specialist firm for fumigation. This is also your best option if the piece has been seriously weakened or has a rare and special finish which might easily be damaged by liquid treatment.

Matching mini-patterned paper and fabrics are used for ceiling, walls and bed curtains in this light and airy room. The curtains are suspended from a graceful wooden *couronne* centred over the turn-of-the-century bed. The pale colours of the carpet, walls and curtains make the bed very much the dominant object and show it off to effect.

PAINTINGS, WATERCOLOURS AND DRAWINGS

Once again, environmental conditions are crucial in looking after any works on paper, whether paintings, drawings, watercolours or prints. Paintings, because of the elements which they contain – wood, canvas, pigment, varnish etc. – can be easily damaged by fluctuations of temperature (causing shrinking, distortion, paint cracking), particularly in excessively dry, over-heated homes. When it comes to hanging paintings always avoid positions above radiators, fires or heating vents and in direct sunlight. Extreme dampness, on the other hand, can cause mould and other problems.

The handling of paintings should be done with great care. Try not to touch the surface of a canvas with your fingers and, when transporting paintings, wrap them in bubble paper or cushion them with padding, taking particular care not

125

to damage fragile mouldings on frames. Never try and clean an oil painting yourself, except to dust it extremely lightly with a soft cloth or a very soft brush. You can blow dust from picture frame crevices with a small, clean, dry plastic bottle or hair dryer on a slow, cold setting. If the painting is very dirty, shows signs of mould or the varnish has become extremely discoloured with age, it should be taken to a professional restorer.

Drawings and watercolours are both particularly light-sensitive and must be kept out of direct sunlight. Ultraviolet rays can damage paper and watercolours and ink can fade if left exposed. This can occur very quickly, and the entire colour key of a work can be altered in a short time. Pollution and dampness in the atmosphere can damage works of art on paper, as can clumsy handling. All pictures should be hung with quality picture wire rather than with string, which is liable to rot. They should be stored or displayed away from extremes of heat and moisture and checked regularly for signs of deterioration – foxing, mould and insect infestation. If they show such signs, take them to a restorer or conservator at once.

Valuable ceramics are best kept on shelves behind glass-fronted doors. They should never be washed in a dishwasher.

METALS

Different metals have different properties which dictate the appropriate cleaning methods and handling. But all metals – in spite of appearances – are vulnerable to scratching, denting, tarnish and corrosion, the soft metals (e.g. gold and silver) being more vulnerable than the hard (e.g. iron). Generally, the handling of all metalwork, even the dusting of it, should be kept to a minimum, as it is very easy to harm the surface.

Heat, damp and light all accelerate tarnishing, the result of a chemical reaction between the metal and the atmosphere. All metals can, in theory, be safely cleaned with

proprietary polishes and cleaners if the manufacturer's instructions are followed (the chemicals they contain pose safety hazards if used incorrectly). However, since all polishing is abrasive and will eventually wear down the surface of any metal object, only do it when absolutely necessary. Most metals will corrode in damp conditions and even the touch of a bare hand is enough to cause a metal to tarnish. Whereas some surface corrosion actually protects the metal (for example, the vibrant green oxidation on copper roofs or the browny-green patination on bronze statues), other types of corrosion (such as rust) can build up and eat into metals. The important thing is to identify the type of metal you are dealing before you start cleaning and to seek professional advice when in doubt.

Remember, if you are polishing any metal inlays in furniture or other objects, to take extreme care not to let the polish get on to the surrounding wood or surface. Wherever possible, it is better simply to polish lightly with a soft, clean cloth. Also be careful when washing floors to avoid wetting brass threshold strips because, once tarnished, they become difficult to clean. If you are using polish on them, protect the surrounding floor surface by putting brown paper or a cloth of some kind.

GLASS

Because of its obvious fragility, glass needs the greatest care in handling. Most glass can be washed by hand with a mild detergent. Old glass should never be put in the dishwasher as it may chip, develop surface cracks with the heat, or get a milky 'bloom'. It is advisable not to use proprietary glass cleaners on old glass mirrors: these contain chemicals which may cause damage to the glass or to its frame. Instead,

dust and polish the mirrors with a clean, soft cloth. White spirit added to the water can be applied to lift greasy dirt, but make sure the liquid does not touch the frame.

Glass chandeliers can be dusted from a step ladder, but if you need to clean them they have to be dismantled (the electricity having been turned off at the mains first!). Take great care to identify each piece as it comes down or you will forget how to put it together again.

CERAMICS

Like glass, ceramics can obviously be easily broken and chipped by clumsy handling and poor storage and display. If you do have an accident with a valuable object, do not try to glue it yourself as this might further damage the broken edges. Instead the pieces should be carefully collected and taken to a professional for repair.

Like most antiques, ceramics should be handled as little as possible. Be careful how you pick up an object to move or dust it, remembering that there may be more than one part to it (for example, lids or other loose bits). When it comes to cleaning, you must again identify the type of ceramic. Hard-paste ceramics can – provided they are in perfect condition – be washed with care and in a mild detergent solution, but *never* in a dishwasher. Soft-paste porcelain should *never* be immersed in water. Instead these types should be cleaned with damp cotton buds and dried quickly. Also never wash any piece that has chips, flaking surfaces or loose pigments. Water can also do damage to unglazed ceramics with a porous body and to any piece that is cracked or held together with metal rivets.

BOOKS

Books – in particular old cloth and leather books – should be handled

with great care; it is easy to damage them, especially when pulling them out of a bookshelf. Direct light and changes in temperature can also cause damage to books, as can water and the ravages of insects and mice. Store books in bookshelves in as protected a spot as possible, taking care not to wedge them in too tightly, as this damages their spines and puts a strain on the joints of the binding. There needs to be a certain amount of moisture in the atmosphere to prevent the books' paper from becoming brittle, but inadequate ventilation could lead to mould or the right conditions for such pests as silverfish, woodworm and other insects. Regular inspection for all signs of damage is the only answer.

The best way to clean books is to take them out of the bookshelf and dust them gently along the top edge away from the spine with a clean duster or soft brush. Never be tempted to vacuum along bookshelves or you may lose bits of the spine or jacket (always keep dust jackets on books). Similarly, never bang the covers of a book together to release the dust. The old-fashioned leather or cloth fringes that used to be fixed to the edges of bookshelves were useful as they automatically dusted the tops of books as they were withdrawn from the shelf – an idea that should definitely be revived.

In the case of valuable antique books, all repairs (even if minor, such as a detached binding or a torn page) should be undertaken by a professional. Likewise, it is best to have any leather dressing of the binding carried out professionally, rather than to attempt it yourself.

OVERLEAF: Collections of beautifully bound books, as in the bookshelves here, need to be kept in optimal conditions if they are to be adequately preserved.

PRACTICAL
tips

*H*owever large or small the job you are undertaking, it helps to have a few practical basics under your belt. 'In the Beginning' (pp.21–31) discussed the need to establish a framework for your decorative scheme; in this section I shall concentrate on simple, technical tasks, such as measuring for upholstery, curtains and blinds, choosing bulb types and hanging pictures successfully. Anyone can grasp these essentials – the tips I offer are simply a reminder of a number of common-sense practices.

ROOM PLANNING

On these two pages are the symbols most commonly used on architectural plans to denote the positions of windows, doors, radiators, light fittings, switches and different electrical (and gas) points. Also shown are the kind of shorthand sketches used to depict pieces of furniture. By drawing these objects to scale on your room plans, you can see exactly how much space each piece will take up. You can then determine whether an object will fit gracefully into the room in which you would like it to

go, or whether you should reconsider its position. It will also become apparent how much other furniture can or cannot be fitted in. To aid this exercise you could cut pieces of paper into different furniture shapes so that they may be easily juggled around on the plans. You will inevitably find room planning using a grid and these outline drawings to be an indispensable tool for accurate room design. This method should obviate many common mistakes, such as buying oversize furniture and appliances.

On the following pages (pp. 132-3) is a grid on which you may make an accurate room plan (see also pp. 24-5).

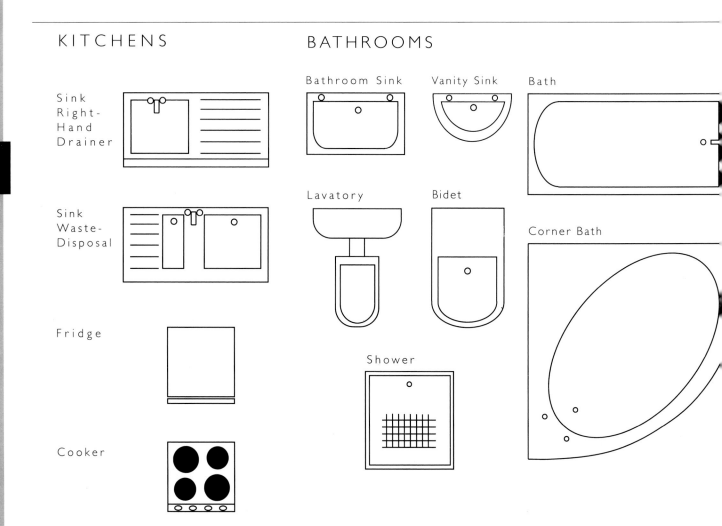

KITCHENS

Sink
Right-
Hand
Drainer

Sink
Waste-
Disposal

Fridge

Cooker

BATHROOMS

Bathroom Sink

Vanity Sink

Bath

Lavatory

Bidet

Corner Bath

Shower

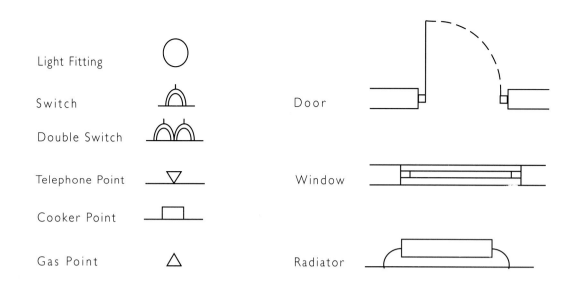

Light Fitting

Switch

Double Switch

Telephone Point

Cooker Point

Gas Point

Door

Window

Radiator

BEDROOMS   LIVING ROOMS

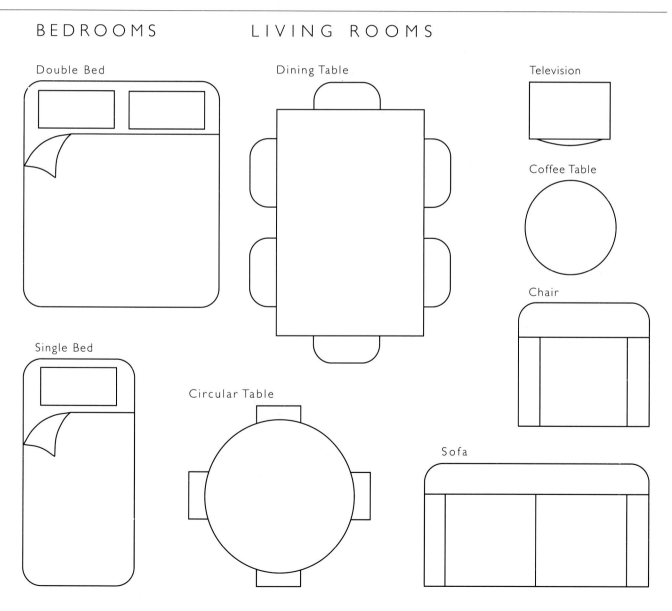

Double Bed

Dining Table

Television

Coffee Table

Chair

Single Bed

Circular Table

Sofa

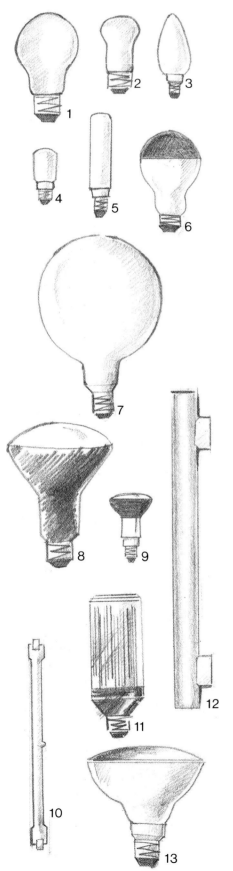

LIGHTING

Over the last decade or so there has been an enormous increase in the choice of bulbs available, and indeed, the choice of different types of light, with a vast range of fluorescent and halogen bulbs to choose from. In fact, the big news in lighting is undoubtedly the vast improvement in fluorescent bulbs, which are now able to provide a much warmer, more pleasant quality of light. As is well-known, they are also highly efficient, their energy-saving credentials helping to give them a greater penetration into the mass-market. The only problems facing the consumer are, how to discriminate between all these different bulbs and which bulb should be used for which fixture. On this page is illustrated a selection of tungsten or incandescent, halogen and fluorescent bulbs.

1	General-purpose tungsten bulb
2–5	Decorative tungsten bulbs
6	Crown-silvered tungsten bulb
7	Round (globe) tungsten bulb
8–9	Tungsten reflector bulbs
10	Linear tungsten-halogen floodlighting bulb
11	Miniature fluorescent long-life bulb
12	Tungsten strip
13	Parabolic aluminized reflector (PAR) lamp
14–16	Fluorescent strips
17	Fluorescent U-lamp
18	Circular fluorescent light
19	Single-ended tubular halogen lamp
20	Standard-voltage single-ended tubular halogen lamp.
21	Low-voltage miniature halogen lamp
22	Halogen reflector lamp (cool beam)

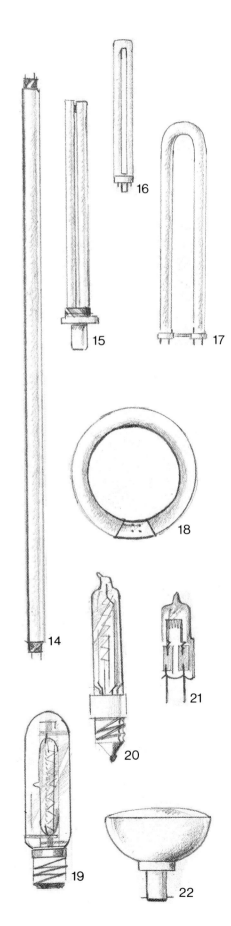

HANGING PICTURES

When you are hanging groups of pictures it usually helps first to lay them out on the floor underneath the wall where you propose to hang them. This way you can shuffle them around until you think you have found the best arrangement, without making unfortunate marks on the wall. You should, of course, try to preserve a sense of balance and proportion with the other objects in the room, remembering that vertical arrangements will make a room seem higher and horizontal ones will help to make walls seem longer.

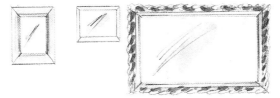

STRAIGHT LINE

This is a classic arrangement with the largest painting placed centrally, balanced by smaller pictures on either side. Notice that, even though the smaller pictures are of different shapes, their scale is sufficiently similar to allow a harmonious grouping with enough variety to keep it from looking dull.

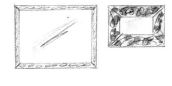

DIAGONAL LINE

These two groupings (left and right) have an imaginary diagonal line drawn across them. Oval, square and rectangular frames are arranged within a rectangular space, the sides, bottoms and tops of frames aligning as if within a disciplined frame themselves. These sorts of arrangements look good over a side-table, and are an excellent way to show off disparate groups of objects.

CLASSIC AND SQUARE

A classic arrangement (left) is to balance a large picture with two small ones or to balance four similarly sized pictures in a block. This is invariably more attractive than a simple side-by-side formation. The square arrangement (right) could equally contain an assortment of objects, as well as pictures.

TRIANGLE AND INVERTED TRIANGLE

Another lively way to present a group of differently sized pictures is to imagine a triangular shape pointing up or down. If the point is to the top, the smaller pictures should be placed above the larger. It follows then that, when the point is to the bottom, the smaller pictures are best placed beneath those that are larger. Either variant has the effect of heightening a wall.

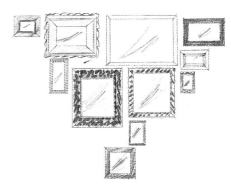

Clearly you should be conversant with the style of window treatment you want before you measure up a window. Headings, in particular, can make quite a difference to the meterage or yardage required. Once you have chosen a style, you must also think, if you intend to have curtains, of what length will be most practical and aesthetically desirable. You might not, for example, want to put long, trailing curtains into a small child's room, or a room which dogs and cats frequent. These reservations aside, curtains generally look better puddling slightly on to, or just touching the floor (unless you have tiny windows, in which case sill-length is preferable). Alternatively, you might like to consider a fabric blind (or shade), or other types of blinds or shutters. Whatever you choose, it is vital to know the depth of the treatment, and to remember that, if you decide to use a fabric with any sort of repeat pattern, you will need to allow for the repeats in the length of the fabric. Measuring a repeat means measuring the length of a complete design or motif before it occurs again, the implication of which is that you generally have to allow rather more material for a patterned fabric than you would for a plain. Incidentally, if you are going to have floor-length curtains, it is usual to start with a full repeat just below the heading, whereas for short curtains and fabric blinds (or shades) the full repeat is normally positioned at the bottom. On matching windows the repeats should be identical.

An expandable metal or wooden rule is generally far more useful than a fabric tape-measure which is liable to stretch and distort. Always measure from the top of the window to wherever you want the treatment to finish, and measure the width of the window (or the length of the track or pole) carefully, particularly if you intend to take the curtains past the edge of the frame. Don't forget to allow for good hems in case of shrinkage when the fabric is cleaned.

MEASURING FOR WINDOW TREATMENTS

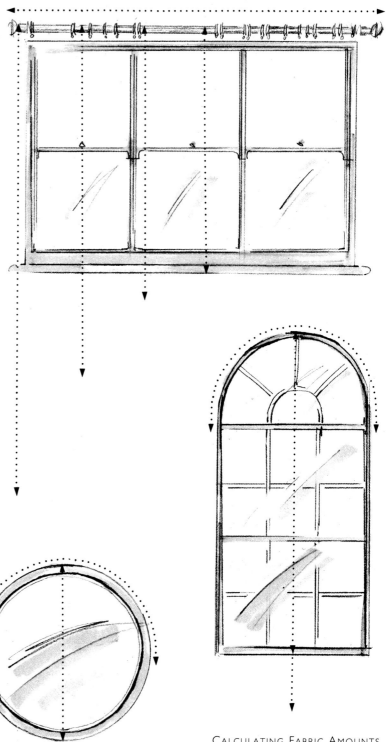

CALCULATING FABRIC AMOUNTS
Try to choose a fabric the width of which is appropriate to the span of the window. To calculate how many fabric widths you will need you must divide the total desired width of the curtain (or shade or blind) by the width of your chosen fabric, always rounding up the total and remembering to take repeats into account.

BLINDS

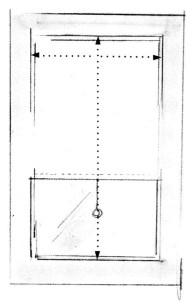

ROMAN BLINDS (OR SHADES)

Roman blinds are popular because they look tailored, but are generally dressier than roller blinds and have accordion-like folds, which vary in size from 5cm (2ins) to 10cm (4 ins). These folds can be soft and unconstructed looking, or crisp and neat. Roman blinds appear flat when down, like roller blinds, and fold only when raised. The pleated folds then fall both to the front and back. A variation is the gathered Roman blind which is shirred along the sides and sometimes in vertical rows. All of them are fixed from a length of battening, either fitted to the ceiling of a recessed window or mounted on supports set above the window. Measure width and depth as for roller blinds.

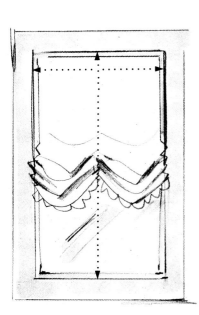

ROLLER BLINDS (OR SHADES)

Roller blinds are usually made of straight lengths of laminated or stiffened fabric fixed to a spring-tension roller, or operated with a ball-and-chain cord. If the windows are deeply recessed, they are generally positioned against the glass, but where there is no recess they are best mounted on the window frame (if it is wooden and flat enough to take the fixings), or on the wall. They may also be reverse-mounted, whereby the roller is to the back of the blind. First measure the width of the area to be covered, remembering to allow 1.5cm (⅝ in) at each side for the pin-and-spring mechanism. Then measure the drop of the blind from the top of the roller.

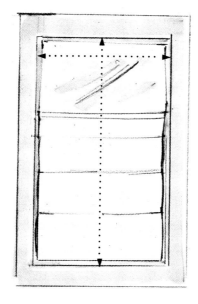

AUSTRIAN BLINDS (OR SHADES)

The ruched look of Austrian blinds is achieved by vertical shirring every 7.5 to 30cm (3 to 12ins) so that the fabric folds into gentle scallops. This type of blind is often combined with a fringe or ruffles, and may also be box-pleated, or 'ballooned' as in balloon blinds. Headings can be straight, smocked, shirred or pleated, and very short Austrian blinds in themselves make elegant valance treatments or headings over curtains. They are usually mounted on to narrow braid secured into the window frame, wall or ceiling. A variation of the Austrian blind – the festoon, or Parisian – is tightly gathered along the top, rather than sewn with tape.

Measuring Hints

✔ Before your measure, ensure that the track or pole is in its correct position.

✔ Remember that your aim is to work out the area that has to be covered when curtains are drawn or blinds down.

✔ When using fabric, always make allowances for a deep hem – 15–25cm (6–10ins) both at the bottom and sides of the material.

✔ Use an expandable metal or wooden ruler.

✔ Measure the depth – from the top of the track or just beneath the pole to the deepest point of the window treatment.

✔ Measure the width either within the window recess or above, slightly overlapping it.

MEASURING TABLES FOR TABLECLOTHS

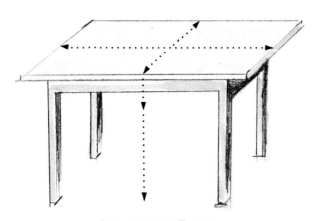

RECTANGULAR TABLES

Measure the dimensions of the tabletop, adding twice the length of the over-hang required to each measurement.

CIRCULAR TABLES

Measure the diameter of the tabletop, adding twice the length of the over-hang required to this measurement.

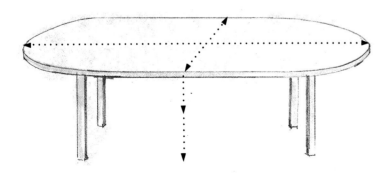

OVAL TABLES

Measure the length and width of the tabletop at the greatest points, adding twice the length of the overhang required to each measurement.

MEASURING UPHOLSTERY

Slip-or loose-covers are useful on so many counts. They not only preserve the pristine state of new upholstery and protect it from the ravages of pets and young children, but can also cover the shabbiness of old upholstery, giving it a new lease of life. An original fabric which might be wrong for a new scheme can be disguised and covers of different weights and colours can freshen up a room in summer or warm it up in winter. Anyone skilled with a needle and a sewing machine can usually run slip-covers up at home, using a material that is washable, or at least dry-cleanable. The real trick to using covers sucessfully lies in correctly measuring and cutting accurate patterns, and first time cover-makers are therefore strongly advised to stick to plain fabrics or allover patterns since it requires a degree of skill to manipulate large repeats. It is essential to be clear in your mind as to the style of cover you intend to make. Do you want it to be loose or crisp like normal upholstery? If your preference is for the latter, be warned that covers can shrink during cleaning. If you want to finish the piece with box pleats or frills, remember too that these variations will require more fabric.

It is advisable first to make a pattern from calico or an old pair of double sheets. After you have noted the measurements of the various sections of a chair or sofa on a rough sketch of the relevant piece, cut the calico or sheet to these measurements, allowing an extra 2cm (¾ in) for seams and 15 cm (6 ins) for tuck-ins at the inside back and seat area. Place these cut-out pieces of calico over the chair or sofa, one area at a time, securing them with sticky tape or upholstery pins. Carefully draw a pencil outline of the actual edge of the section you are working on. Remove the pieces of calico and cut these following the outline, but again allowing for the seams and tuck-ins. As each area is cut out, put the textile back on to the chair to ensure that the pencil outline has been accurate. When all sections are complete, pin the pieces together and join them with tacking stitches, labelling each piece with french chalk. The opening should run from a corner at the foot of the back of the chair or sofa to beneath the scroll, or curve, of the arm. Slip the calico over the piece, and when you are satisfied that it fits well, untack the sections of calico so that they may serve as a pattern for the final fabric.

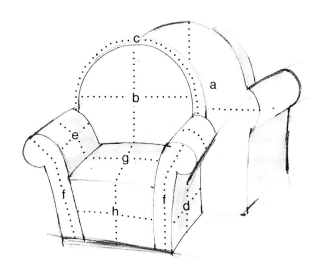

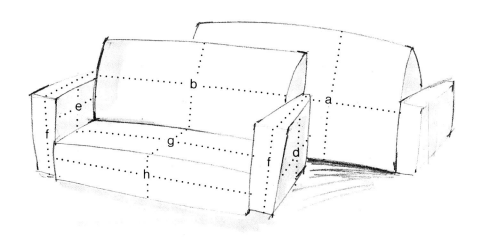

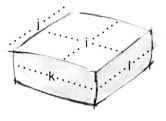

Armchairs and Sofas

Always measure the dimensions of the:

✔ (a) Back*

✔ (b) Inside back

✔ (c) Back box strip

✔ (d) Outside arm

✔ (e) Inside arm*

✔ (f) Arm box strip

✔ (g) Seat*

✔ (h) Front panel

✔ (i) Cushion base and top

✔ (j) Cushion front-gusset strip

✔ (k) Cushion side-gusset strip

✔ (l) Cushion back-gusset strip

* add tuck-in allowance

139

Suppliers of fabric and wallpaper swatches featured on pages 78-83, 97, 110, 114-117:

Sunworthy Wallcoverings
15 Walker Drive
Brampton Ontario
L6T 3Z9 Canada
Telephone: (416) 791-8801
Fax: (416) 791-9972

Design Directions
465 Devon Park
Wayne
PA 19087-1815
Telephone: (800) 722-9255

Walltex Wallcoverings
Borden Consumer Response
180 East Broad Street 35th Floor
Columbus
OH 43215

Pillowtex Corporation / Nettle Creek
4111 Mint Way
Dallas
TX 75237
Telephone: (800) 258-0001 ext. 301

Toli-Matico
55 Mall Drive
Commack
NY 11725

LIVING ROOM

pages 78-79

LEFT TO RIGHT
Sofabed: Nettle Creek, 20512
Slipcover: Nettle Creek, Calico/Wedgewood, IC829
Cushions: Nettle Creek, Light Blue Denim
Flooring: Toli-Matico, vinyl flooring

pages 80-81

LEFT TO RIGHT
Chairs: Nettle Creek Club Chairs, 20071
Slipcover: Nettle Creek, Light blue Denim (as cushions p. 78-9 above)
Chair at desk: antique textile (blue and white regency style)
Wing chair: Nettle Creek, 20070
Curtains and textile of wing chair: Design Directions, Indian Gardens IGF 329, made by Nettle Creek

pages 82-83

LEFT TO RIGHT
Curtains: Design Directions, Sandpiper Edwardian Garden II, MGF 306-24
Dado marbled wallpaper: Design Directions, Faux Finish, FF 127
Rose paint: Benjamin Moore, 4F1286

KITCHEN

pages 96-97

LEFT TO RIGHT
Wallpaper border: Design Directions, Victorian Garden, VG215-02
Kitchen wallpaper: Sunworhy, Mrs. Mitchell's Country, MK 2640
Shelf paper (not visible in photograph, lining suggesion for cupboards): Design Directions, Faux Finishes, FF310-01

BEDROOM

pages 110-111

TOP LEFT
Queen-size bedhead: Nettle Creek, HDB 62
Cover: Design Directions, Indian Gardens, IGF 312

TOP RIGHT
Queen-size bedpread: Nettle Creek, Alpine Syle
Bedspread textile: Design Directions, Indian Gardens, IGF 304

BOTTOM LEFT
Wallpaper: Design Directions, Indian Gardens, 130
Wallpaper border: Design Directions, Bengal, IA 1080

BOTTOM RIGHT
'Four-poster' textile: Nettle Creek, Amara Blue Voile, 626949

CHILDREN'S ROOM

pages 114-115

LEFT TO RIGHT
Blinds (or shades): Sunworthy, Collins AnJu Woodridge 27
Wallpaper: Sunworthy, Cushing LMR 489
Ceiling paper: Sunworthy, LMR 490
Blue paint: Benjamin Moore

pages 115-116

LEFT TO RIGHT
Wallpaper (beneath chair rail): Walltex, OH 515
Cushion: Nettle Creek, Light Blue Denim (as cushions p. 78-9 above)
Covers: J.C. Penney, peach colour
Sisal matting: standard quality available from most floorcovering suppliers.

ACKNOWLEDGMENTS

8 La Maison de Marie Claire (Bailache/Ardouin); 9 above Andreas von Einsiedel/Elizabeth Whiting & Associates/; 9 centre IPC Magazines Limited 1991/Robert Harding Syndication; 9 below La Maison de Marie Claire (Chabaneix/Comte); 10-11 Paul Ryan/J.B.Visual Press; 12 Photography Richard Weidland, Courtesy Belle Magazine; 13 Noelle Hoeppe; 14-15 René Stoeltie; 16 Camera Press; 17 above Chris Mead; 17 below Nadia Mackenzie; 18 Yves Duronsoy; 20 Jan Baldwin; 21 above Jean-Pierre Godeaut; 21 centre Jean Pierre-Godeaut; 21 below Guy Bouchet; 22 above Fritz von der Schulenburg (Franceso Miani d'Angoris); 22 Trevor Richards; 23 Ianthe Ruthven; 26-27 Rodney Hyett/Elizabeth Whiting & Associates; 29 Caroline White; 30 Jean-Pierre Godeaut; 32 Antoine Rozes; 33 above IPC Magazines Limited 1989/Robert Harding Syndication; 33 centre Christian Sarramon; 33 below Nadia Mackenzie; 34 Guy Bouchet; 36-37 La Maison de Marie Claire (Chabaneix/Comte/Postic); 37 above Yves Duronsoy; 37 centre Paul Ryan/J.B. Visual Press; 37 below La Maison de Marie Claire (Snitt/Rozensztroch); 38-39 La Maison de Marie Claire (Nicolas/Postic); 39 below Nadia Mackenzie; 40 Vogue Living (Rodney Weidland); 42 Yves Duronsoy; 43 Antoine Rozes/Stylograph; 44-45 Houses & Interiors; 46 centre Fritz von der Schulenburg (David Hicks International); 46 right Caroline White; 47 Fritz von der Schulenburg (John McCall); 48 Nadia Mackenzie; 49 above Piet von Brockelen; 49 centre Christian Sarramon; 49 below Jean-Pierre Godeaut; 50 Paul Ryan/J.B. Visual Press; 51 Jeremy Cockayne; 52-53 above Yves Duronsoy; 54 Guy Bouchet; 56 Nadia Mackenzie; 57 David Phelps; 58 Paul Ryan/International Interiors; 61 Rodney Hyett/Elizabeth Whiting & Associates; 62 left Yves Duronsoy; 63 Di Lewis/Elizabeth Whiting & Associates; 64 Fritz von der Schulenburg (Franceso Miani d'Angoris); 66 Ianthe Ruthven; 67 Fritz von der Schulenburg (Andrew Wadsworth); 67 centre Shona Wood (John, Meryl and Rosie Lakin); 67 below Christian Sarramon; 68 Antoine Rozes; 69 Jean-Pierre Godeaut; 70 June Buck/Elizabeth Whiting & Associates; 71 Paul Ryan/J.B. Visual Press; 72-72 Jean-Pierre Godeaut; 74 Camera Press; 75 Yves Duronsoy; 76 Christian Sarramon; 84-85 Camera Press; 86 David Phelps; 88 Paul Ryan/J.B. Visual Press; 89 Fritz von der Schulenburg; 91 above Jacques Primois/Stylograph; 91 below Rodney Hyett/Elizabeth Whiting & Associates; 92 John Hollingshead; 93 Rene Stoeltie; 94 John Hollingshead; 98 Fritz von der Schulenburg; 99 Yves Duronsoy; 100-101 Ianthe Ruthven; 102 Christian Sarramon; 103 Guy Bouchet; 104 Vogue Living (Ross Honeysett); 105 Yves Duronsoy; 106 above Paul Ryan/J.B. Visual Press; 106 below Christian Sarramon; 107 above Fritz von der Schulenburg (Mimi O'Connell); 107 below Yves Duronsoy; 108 Fritz von der Schulenburg (Joanna Wood); 113 above Fritz von der Schulenburg; 113 below Camera Press; 118 Vogue Living (Anthony Browell); 119 above Antoine Rozes; 119 centre Houses & Interiors; 119 below Dia Press; 123 Paul Ryan/International Interiors; 124 Marcus Harrison; 125 Camera Press; 126 Ingrid Mason Pictures/Marie Louise Avery; 128 Fritz von der Schulenburg;

Special photography by Kurt Dolnier/Lightfall Photographic: 6-7, 46 left, 52 below, 62 right, 78-83, 96-97, 110-111, 114-117

AUTHOR'S ACKNOWLEDGMENTS

I have so many people to thank for their invaluable help with this book. I have especially appreciated the patience, tact and scholarship of my editor, Peggy Vance; the talent and skills of the designer, Ruth Prentice; the cheerful attention to detail of Abigail Ahern, Julia Pashley, Alison McIver, Sarah Riddell, Andrew Steeds and Emma Wheeler; the support always given by Mary Evans and Anne Furniss, and the backing of my publishers, Alison Cathie and Ray Roberts. If I had not had the inestimable luck to get to know Barbara Prisco, my working life would have been considerably less easy, so special thanks are due to her.

My warmest gratitude to all who worked with me on the US television series, *Decorating with Mary Gilliatt*, particularly my producer, colleague and friend Sue Breger and her husband Dr Herb Breger – for their perserverance and faith; to Polly Kosko for her warmth and special vision; to Sidney Palmer, Jim Eddins, Tom Clark and Jean Pinkston whom I value as much for their friendship as for their talents, and all the rest of my friends at SCETV. I was very lucky to benefit from the help of the aforementioned Barbara Prisco on this project too, as I was to have the gifted services of our set designer Gordon Juel, and all the hard work was made pleasurable with the extra help and humour of Elsie Taylor Stanley and Sandy Dolnier. Finally my deepest thanks to Blake Perkins, Ethan Corrigan and Ridgley Bullock who literally got everything going for me.